Curriculum Provision
for the
Gifted and Talented
in the **Primary School**

English, Maths, Science and ICT

Edited by
**Deborah Eyre &
Lynne McClure**

 **David Fulton** Publishers

in association with
The National Association for Able Children in Education

David Fulton Publishers Ltd
414 Chiswick High Road, London W45TF

www.fultonpublishers.co.uk

First published in Great Britain by David Fulton Publishers 2001

Note: The right of Deborah Eyre and Lynne McClure to be identified as the authors of this work has been asserted by them in accordance with the Copyright, Designs and Patents Act 1988.

Copyright © Deborah Eyre and Lynne McClure 2001

British Library Cataloguing in Publication Data
A catalogue record for this book is available from the British Library.

ISBN 1–85346–771–5

Typeset by Textype Typesetters, Cambridge
Printed in Great Britain

Curriculum Provision
for the
Gifted and Talented
in the **Primary School**

Contents

Preface

The last three years have seen the issue of education for able/gifted pupils move from the margins of the educational arena and towards centre stage. The dismantling of the 'Assisted Places Scheme' occurred in 1997 along with a government commitment to the establishment of a national strategy to help gifted and talented pupils in maintained schools to make the most of their educational opportunities. The national strategy is being developed using a two-stranded approach. The first strand is a national pilot project, located in inner cities as part of the Excellence in Cities initiative. In this strand schools are required to have a policy on gifted and talented pupils, a designated member of staff taking responsibility for gifted and talented pupils and a distinct teaching and learning programme for the cohort in question. The second strand involves a greater recognition of the needs of gifted and talented pupils within wider educational initiatives such as the literacy and numeracy strategies.

The need for schools to look more closely at their provision for the able, or, to use the adopted government terminology, 'gifted and talented' children, has been evident for many years. In 1992 HMI stated:

> Very able pupils in maintained schools primary and secondary schools are insufficiently challenged by the work they are set.

Five years later, and after a period of immense change in education, OFSTED found that the problem of underachievement among the more able was still a feature of education in many schools:

> Provision for very able children, defined as the top 5% by attainment, is a significant weakness in one-third of maintained primary schools and about 30% of maintained secondary schools. (OFSTED internal report 1997, quoted in House of Commons 1999).

Many reasons have been put forward for the lack of effective provision for able/gifted pupils including comprehensive education, the National Curriculum, the British attitude to academic excellence, the private school system etc. All these are possible factors, but in practical terms the most compelling reason seems to be that over a significant period of time educationalists did not see this as an important issue. Few schools systematically addressed the needs of their able pupils and, for those who did, guidance on how to make improvements was in short supply.

An inquiry from the House of Commons Education Select Committee (House of Commons 1999) identified five main problems with provision:

- the needs of children of high ability are not seen as a priority by teachers and schools;
- schools do not set high enough levels of expectation for their pupils;
- the ethos of schools (and, more widely, society) does not value high academic or intellectual achievement;
- teachers are unsure about the most effective ways of recognising high potential or of teaching the most able children; and
- resources for providing the best education for such children are not available.

Since this report the Department for Education and Employment (DfEE), and other government agencies, have gone some way towards addressing these issues. The Excellence in Cities pilot provides inservice training for coordinators of gifted and talented pupils as well as resources for developing more effective school-based provision. National guidance on meeting the needs of the gifted and talented has also been produced by the Qualifications and Curriculum Authority (QCA) and additional material linked to the literacy and numeracy strategies has been produced. The needs of the gifted and talented are being given greater priority in schools and it is likely that standards will rise accordingly.

Much has been written internationally regarding the educational and social needs of gifted children, but relatively little research and publication has taken place in the United Kingdom (UK). In 1998 OFSTED commissioned a review of the international literature (Freeman 1998) to provide an overview of what has been learnt. This document is particularly helpful in considering the psychological literature related to the nature of giftedness but perhaps less helpful to the teacher in securing a whole-school approach to effective educational provision. This is not a criticism of the document itself, but rather a recognition of the inherent weakness in reviews of this type; because educational systems vary greatly, educational provision, which must take account of the general educational context, will vary too.

The international research base has, however, been essential in providing a theoretical basis for school-focused research in England and for exploring effective provision in relation to the English educational context. Since the 1980s small scale work has occurred in England. During the 1990s a range of small scale, school-focused research projects have been undertaken by researchers, resulting in the production of guidance to teachers, (Clark and Callow 1998, Koshy and Casey 1998, Kennard 1996 and Lee-Corbin and Denicolo 1998).

My own guidance book *Able Children in Ordinary Schools* (Eyre 1997) was based on the outcomes of ten years of school-focused research working with teachers in Oxfordshire LEA schools, and it provides comprehensive guidance to schools on the establishment of a whole-school approach to the education of able pupils. This new book explores more fully the issues related to teaching particular subjects in the primary school and is the result of work undertaken by colleagues in the Research Centre for Able Pupils (ReCAP) at Westminster Institute of Education, Oxford Brookes University. ReCAP is now the country's largest research centre for able pupils and is at the forefront of work on gifted children and their education.

Deborah Eyre
April 2001

References

Clack, C. and Callow, F. (1998) *Education Able Children*. London: David Fulton Publishers.

Eyre, D. (1997) *Able Children in Ordinary Schools*. London: David Fulton Publishers.

Freeman, J. (1998) *Educating the Very Able: Current International Research*. London: HMSO.

HMI (1992) *Education Observed: The Education of Very Able Children in Maintained Schools*. London: HMSO.

House of Commons (1999) Education and Employment Committee. Third Report, 'Highly Able Children'. London: HMSO.

Kennard, R. (1996) *Teaching Mathematically Able Children*. Oxford: NACE (National Association for Able Children in Education).

Koshy, V. and Casey, R. (1998) *Effective Provision for Able and Exceptionally Able Children*. London: Hodder and Stoughton.

Lee-Corbin, H. and Denicolo, P. (1998) *Able Children in Primary Schools*. London: David Fulton Publishers.

**THE NATIONAL ASSOCIATION FOR
ABLE CHILDREN IN EDUCATION**
PO Box 242, Arnolds Way,
Oxford OX2 9FR

Registered Charity No. 327230

Tel: 01865 861879
e-mail: info@nace.co.uk

Fax: 01865 861880
www.nace.co.uk

MISSION STATEMENT

NACE . . . the association of professionals, promoting and supporting the education of able and talented children.

AIMS

1. To promote the fact that able and talented children have particular educational needs that must be met to realise their full potential.

2. To be proactive in promoting discussion and debate by raising appropriate issues in all educational forums and through liaison with educational policy makers.

3. To encourage commitment to the personal, social and intellectual development of the whole child.

4. To encourage a broad, balanced and appropriate curriculum for able and talented children.

5. To encourage the use of a differentiated educational provision in the classroom through curriculum enrichment and extension.

6. To make education an enjoyable, exciting and worthwhile experience for the able and talented child.

OBJECTIVES

1. To promote the development, implementation and evaluation in all schools of a coherent policy for able and talented children.
2. To provide appropriate support, resources and materials for the education of able and talented children.
3. To provide methods of identification and support to the education community.
4. To provide and facilitate appropriate initial teacher training.
5. To stimulate, initiate and coordinate research activities.
6. To develop a national base and establish regional centres.

STATEMENT

To make education an enjoyable, exciting and worthwhile experience for able and talented children.

Introduction

The purpose of this book is to assist primary schools in making effective provision for gifted and talented children. The House of Commons (1999) found that teachers were unsure about the most effective ways of recognising high potential or teaching the most able. In recent years, a number of good books have been published which help schools to understand the general principles behind making effective provision and also the management implications for schools. In this book we have chosen to focus specifically on a more detailed examination of curriculum provision. This is, in part, because the majority of time spent in primary school is devoted to delivery of the core National Curriculum areas and, in part, because schools working to improve their provision for the gifted have highlighted the need for more detailed guidance in these areas.

New ideas on the education of the gifted

Educational provision for gifted pupils should reflect our understanding of what it means to be gifted. In this book we draw on the latest research into giftedness and consider its implications for school-based planning. We also link the research findings to the current educational context in primary schools and highlight the opportunities offered by the National Curriculum and the literacy and numeracy strategies.

The scope and organisation of the book

This book is divided into six chapters. The first chapter looks at what schools should be trying to achieve and why. It draws on the substantial research base existing internationally and applies the findings to the context of English primary schools. It deals in some detail with the complex issue of identification and its implications for curriculum planning. New ideas on giftedness have emerged in recent years which point to the developmental nature of giftedness and the differences in the educational needs of gifted children in the Foundation Stage, Key Stage 1 and Key Stage 2. In this chapter, Eyre covers the latest research on this along with thoughts on its significance.

Chapter 2 focuses on English in the primary school and on the literacy strategy. The chapter highlights the fact that linguistic ability is often recognised early in a child's life and significant achievements can occur before a child comes to school. Holderness therefore encourages schools to anticipate the arrival of very able language users and to base subsequent provision on a detailed assessment of existing skills. This chapter is full of ideas for providing challenge in the classroom in all stages of the primary school and in all areas of English.

Chapter 3 looks at maths in the primary school. It considers what it means to be gifted in mathematics and how schools might recognise gifted mathematicians. Once again the developmental nature of giftedness is explored; but this time in relation to maths. The various possible approaches to meeting the needs of able mathematicians are examined by McClure and ideas are given for classroom activities.

Chapter 4 considers science and its role in helping children to develop as sophisticated thinkers. Coates and Wilson stress an enquiry based approach to science and highlight the gains for able children when science moves beyond the teaching of facts and begins to explore ideas through the introduction of such techniques as cognitive conflict. Practical ideas on how to present classroom tasks are linked to examples of how to use questioning as a technique for creating challenge.

Chapter 5 explores the role of ICT as a learning tool for the gifted and talented. ICT is often seen as a way of creating challenge for the gifted. In this chapter Higgins looks at the various ways in which ICT can be used and also highlights some of the risks and limitations. Specific ideas for use in the classroom are identified, including LOGO and hypermedia.

Chapter 6 summarises the findings from the book and offers conclusions.

Reference

House of Commons (1999) Education and Employment Committee, Third Report, 'Highly Able Children'. London: HMSO.

Contributors to the book

Deborah Eyre is head of ReCAP (Research Centre for Able Pupils) and also deputy head of the Westminster Institute of Education. She is a former school coordinator and Local Education Authority (LEA) adviser for able pupils and has worked extensively with schools on improving educational provision for able pupils. Her research interests lie in pedagogy and classroom practice and in particular the ways in which teachers can 'tinker' with their existing practice to create a classroom more conducive to the development of high ability. She has published three books on able pupils as well as variety of papers and chapters. Deborah is a past President of NACE (National Association for Able Children in Education), a member of the government advisory group for gifted and talented, specialist adviser to the House of Commons Education Select Committee for its Highly Able Children inquiry and a consultant to QCA.

Jackie Holderness has worked in primary education for over 20 years. She taught at the British School in the Netherlands, where she was primary language coordinator and editor of the school magazine. Before joining Oxford Brookes, as a specialist in language and literature in education, she was a deputy head teacher in Oxfordshire. She is a qualified OFSTED inspector for the nursery and primary stages. She is currently Course Leader of the MA in Education for International Schools. She regularly contributes to professional development courses at home and overseas.

She has published English for Young Learners (EFL) materials and written books for British teachers. Her main professional interests are: the use of story in learning; teaching gifted children; learning how to learn and accelerated learning; the teaching of writing and poetry and teachers' use of action research and professional development.

Lynne McClure is researching the provision of maths enrichment activities for able Year 6 pupils and is working with colleagues in both primary and secondary partnership schools on the development of a series of maths masterclasses. As a founder member of the Mathematically Promising Network, Lynne is involved in the development of a cross-curricular website for teachers of able pupils.

Lynne is project leader for the primary Excellence in Cities Gifted and Talented Coordinators' Training Programme and the training programme for Responsible Teachers. She also teaches on various CPD programmes within the centre and lectures in mathematics on the institute's PGCE course. Her teaching and management experience includes primary, secondary, adult basic education, Further Education (FE) and Higher Education (HE).

David Coates undertakes work for ReCAP in science and technology in the primary school. He is evaluating the contribution of INPUT (Industrial Project for Understanding Technology) to the education of able primary children in the region. He is involved in a collaborative action research project with other members of the ReCAP team and primary teachers in Oxfordshire, using a case study approach to evaluate effective classroom based strategies used with able pupils.

David is a senior lecturer in science and design and technology education at Westminster Institute. He has taught in both secondary and primary schools before entering higher education. His research interests include the identification and development of investigative skills in science with Early Years children and the use of questioning to develop children's higher order thinking skills.

Helen Wilson undertakes consultancy and research focusing on able children and science, and runs masterclasses for able primary children. Helen is a member of the team involved in an action research project investigating the characteristics of a successful teacher of able primary pupils. She is currently a senior lecturer in physics to the main science students on the B.Ed course at Westminster Institute and also teaches core knowledge science to the non-science specialists on the B.Ed and PGCE courses. She began her teaching career at King Edward VI High School for Girls in Birmingham, a selective school with highly able pupils, and later taught in a small village primary school.

Chris Higgins undertakes work for ReCAP in Information and Communications Technology (ICT), evaluating the use that able children can make of ICT as a cognitive tool to develop thinking skills and investigating how able children work in an ICT-rich learning environment . He has been involved in the use of ICT in schools since the first introduction of computers into the classroom. His research and writing have concentrated on the use of ICT to enhance teaching and learning at all ages from early years through to higher education, and in all areas of the curriculum. His most recent publication is *ICT in the Primary Classroom: a Teacher's Guide to Enhancing Teaching and Learning* (2001) London: RoutledgeFalmer.

Chris is a senior lecturer in mathematics and ICT coordinator for the Institute. He has taught in the secondary sector and, since 1980, in higher education. He is on the editorial boards of the *Journal for IT in Teacher Education* and *Westminster Studies in Education*, and is a member of the committee of ITTE (the Association for Information Technology in Teacher Education).

CHAPTER 1

An effective primary school for the gifted and talented

Deborah Eyre

A school-wide approach to gifted and talented

This chapter outlines the areas which need to be considered if a school is to improve its provision for the gifted and talented. The gifted and talented are not a homogeneous group and therefore provision needs to be responsive to individual needs and sufficiently flexible to take account of particular ages and contexts. This chapter aims to help schools to understand not only what they should do, but also why it is appropriate and how to tailor the general guidance on provision to fit their own particular context. Finally it provides guidance on how to monitor provision and judge whether the school really is an effective school for gifted and talented children.

For most schools, meeting the needs of their gifted and talented children is part of a commitment to ensuring suitable educational opportunities for all children. Schools are not looking to provide for their gifted and talented at the expense of other children but rather to ensure that all children, including those with gifts and talents, are receiving good quality educational provision. In considering education for gifted and talented children it is not surprising to find that schools who are judged to be successful generally are also most likely to be among those successful in providing for their gifted and talented children. Schools who meet the criteria for effective schools (Sammons, Hillman and Mortimore 1996) are also likely to be effective in meeting the needs of the gifted and talented (see Figure 1.1).

Key point

Meeting the educational needs of the gifted and talented is about building on good general school provision, not about providing something entirely different.

Therefore, in judging the effectiveness of a school in providing for its gifted and talented children, a look at overall school provision is one aspect of the process. For a school to be a good school for the gifted and talented it must first be a good school for the majority. Such factors as systems for assessment, planning and monitoring must exist before they can be modified to meet the needs of the gifted.

Eleven factors for effective schools	
1. Professional leadership	Firm and purposeful A participative approach The leading professional
2. Shared vision and goals	Unity of purpose Consistency of practices Collegiality and collaboration
3. A learning environment	An orderly atmosphere An attractive working environment
4. Concentration on teaching and learning	Maximisation of learning time Academic emphasis Focus on achievement
5. Purposeful teaching	Efficient organisation Clarity of purpose Structured lessons Adaptive practice
6. High expectations	High expectations all round Communicating expectations Providing intellectual challenge
7. Positive reinforcement	Clear and fair discipline Feedback
8. Monitoring progress	Monitoring pupil performance Evaluating school performance
9. Pupils' rights and responsibilities	Raising pupil self-esteem Positions of responsibility Control of work
10. Home-school partnership	Parental involvement in their children's learning
11. A learning organisation	School-based staff development

Figure 1.1 Eleven factors for effective schools

Two more aspects, in addition to those found in any effective school, form the basis of judgements in respect of effective provision: first, the availability of opportunities for challenge and the access of individuals to them, and second, the quality of the opportunities on offer. Do they really present a stimulating and challenging range of opportunities and are all those with the potential to benefit from them able to gain access? This section of the chapter looks briefly at the range of opportunities which should be provided and indicators of quality.

Classroom provision

In the primary school the majority of educational opportunities for gifted and talented children should be available as part of general classroom practice. Kerry and Kerry (2000) describe pedagogy as being the key to able student's teaching and learning, and they assert that the key components to effective classroom provision are:

- defining learning objectives;
- setting effective classroom tasks;
- differentiating work;
- questioning effectively;
- explaining effectively.

In providing well for gifted and talented children a school needs to consider how each of these might operate in respect of those of high ability. When considering learning objectives, more challenging objectives for the most able will be a regular feature of classroom planning. This does not mean that different worksheets always need to be provided for the most able; learning objectives can be linked to understanding of additional or more complex concepts and may be achieved through careful questioning. It does mean that a teacher should be able to demonstrate an understanding of the kinds of approaches that are most likely to provide a challenge and justify the choice of a particular approach in a particular set of circumstances. The following goals for extension tasks (Eyre 1997) provide a useful *aide mémoire*:

- critical thinking;
- creative thinking;
- increased independence;
- problem solving ability;
- reflection;
- self-knowledge.

School-wide opportunities

While much of the provision in curriculum areas will be part of classroom practice, the development of the wider framework of opportunities is likely to be part of a school-wide offer. Good provision for gifted and talented is broad-based and balanced. All children, including the gifted and talented, benefit from access to a wide range of experiences. If, as Gardner (2000) suggests, ability exists in a variety of possible domains, then children need to experience opportunities to operate within those domains if their ability is to be revealed. This is particularly important in the Foundation Stage and Key Stage 1 as a child's interest in particular domains is still at an early stage of formation. In practical terms, the child who hears a steel band perform in school may develop an interest in music which is triggered by this single event. A visit to school from a local historian may, indirectly, lead to a child studying history at university. Some opportunities can only be made available at whole-school level – major drama performances or involvement in clubs and societies. These are an important part of provision for all children and equally important for the gifted. Some children may have gifts in areas which are not catered for in the classroom at all and only catered for at whole-school level, e.g. chess.

School-wide opportunities have always been to some extent dependent on the particular skills and interests of teachers in the school. A good school for the gifted and talented ensures a range of opportunities in different domains. If a school chooses to specialise by, for example, offering outstanding musical opportunities, then they need to ensure that the artistically talented or sporting child can also gain access to high-quality opportunities, whether this is provided within the school or beyond it.

School-wide opportunities might include:

- whole-school drama or musical productions;
- clubs and societies;
- competitions;
- access to experts, e.g. artist in residence or book week;
- residential visits;
- specialist workshops;
- visits and events;
- links with schools in other countries.

School-based enrichment opportunities

These are defined as opportunities that are offered to help selected children who have particular abilities and skills. In the primary school the boundary between that which is offered as a school-wide opportunity and that which is offered to selected groups is often blurred. The school is trying to offer experiences to many but also accelerated skills development for some. When deciding whether a particular opportunity should have open access or be for a selected group this distinction is useful. The purpose and nature of the activity should determine to whom it is offered.

Enrichment programmes invoke strong support and also extensive criticism in the research literature. On the plus side able/gifted pupils do benefit from the stimulation of their intellectual peers (Shore 2000) and increases in pace and complexity are easier to achieve in this kind of context (see Figure 1.2). On the

Advantages	Disadvantages
Some opportunities can only be offered in this form since they are unsuitable for the majority of children.

Pace and complexity can be increased and so greater challenge offered in such sessions.

Gifted children enjoy the stimulation of working with their intellectual peers.

Feelings of intellectual isolation can be reduced through access to such opportunities. | Those who might benefit are not self-evident in the 4–11 age range and provision for some may reduce opportunities for others.

Continuity of provision is difficult and expensive for a school to provide.

Educational benefits only occur if the sessions are well planned, have clear goals and are linked directly to other learning. |

Figure 1.2 Offering enrichment to selected groups of pupils

minus side, no research evidence has proved significant long-term educational impact resulting from withdrawal programmes, although increases in motivation and enjoyment are widely reported (Freeman 1998).

This research is important to note because schools tend to be drawn towards enrichment opportunities as a simple way to make provision, and to offer them without sufficient thought.

Key point

Overall, an effective school may choose to include enrichment for selected children as part of its provision. It will however have addressed the issues related to the rationale for this choice of approach, have clear learning outcomes for the sessions, and have taken into account issues around continuity and progression prior to embarking on the project.

Community-based opportunities

A particular dilemma in the education of the gifted and talented is the extent to which the school is the primary context for the nurturing of abilities or talent. Of course it will never be the sole educator;; even for the most academic of subjects home and school educate the child jointly. However, it is also the case that the school plays relatively little part in the development of some kinds of talent – a child learning karate or ballet may do so entirely in a location outside of school. Bloom (1985) found that some of the adults in his study began the development of their talent or ability in school but all later developed it outside the school context.

In the past, schools have not seen their role in relation to the gifted and talented as extending beyond the school (and advice to parents on home support). *Excellence in Cities* (DfEE 1999), however, gives schools responsibility for alerting children and their parents to opportunities for talent development which exist on a local, regional or national basis. This is particularly important for the development of talents not well catered for in school. Local opportunities may include sports clubs and interest clubs (e.g. chess or archaeology) as well as 'explorers' clubs' which are provided specifically for the gifted and talented. National opportunities include schemes run by museums and art galleries as well as the National Trust, etc. Finally, an increasing number of opportunities are appearing on the Internet, and many families have found sites like 'nrich' to be invaluable in extending opportunities to develop skills in maths.

Key point

An effective school for the gifted and talented publicises local and national opportunities for the development of abilities and talent and alerts parents of children with particular abilities to the opportunities available.

Organisational arrangements

An effective school for the gifted and talented will consider the needs of high ability children when it makes decisions on organisational matters such as pupil grouping or assessment. Opportunities will exist to cater for the needs of able individuals, including the chance to work with others of like ability (even where this necessitates working with older children) and opportunities to access extension papers in SATs. It is likely that, in small or generally low-achieving schools, academically able individuals will be seen as having particular individual needs and their provision and progress will be charted accordingly, e.g. by an Individual Education Plan. In larger schools, setting or pupil grouping arrangements will take account of the needs of the gifted and talented.

Effective schools for gifted and talented may use any form of pupil grouping but are likely to set for maths and literacy by the upper end of the primary school. Setting is not in itself a form of provision for the gifted and talented. Even within a top set, levels of achievement can vary considerably and differentiation will be needed. Setting is also problematic in that it requires a decision to be made about the child's potential for achievement at a time when talent development may be fluid and uneven. Setting does provide a good context for presenting challenging opportunities and gifted children, especially in Key Stage 2, tend to prefer setted groups. However, for those children with latent potential or uneven skills, setting may lead to less challenge or withdrawal of opportunities when they are relegated to a lower set. Research on setting in the secondary school (Ireson and Hallam 1999) suggests that there is a poor correlation between academic ability and sets in some schools, and so setting arrangements need to be monitored carefully.

Social and emotional considerations

Stopper (2000) describes the relationship between intellectual and social/emotional development as complex. Work on definitions of high ability includes the role of emotional states, e.g. motivation, and work on high-achieving adults points to the role of emotional wellbeing in high achievement.

For the young child emotional and intellectual needs are difficult to disentangle. Children need to be confident and secure if they are to strive and take risks. This is the same for gifted and talented children as it is for others. Therefore, any provision made by schools for gifted and talented children should take into account its effect on the child or children. For one child, working with older children might be desirable and enjoyable; for another of similar ability it might be stressful and problematic.

Freeman (1998) is unequivocal in saying: 'There is no reliable scientific evidence to show that exceptionally high ability per se is associated with emotional problems, or that inadequate education results in delinquent or disturbed behaviour.'

In the effective school the social and emotional needs of gifted and talented children are addressed in the same way as they are for other children. Their needs are not necessarily greater but they do exist and intellectual progress should not be at the expense of social and emotional development.

Identification of the gifted and talented

Schools beginning to look at provision for gifted and talented pupils usually expect to adopt the approach which Freeman (1998) refers to as the 'diagnose and treat' approach. Under this system a decision is made as to who might constitute a gifted and/or talented cohort and then consideration is given to the educational treatment they may need. While this appears a logical approach, and one which can certainly constitute a part of effective school provision, it cannot alone lead to effective provision for gifted and talented children and can lead instead to inequality of opportunity.

The main reason why this particular approach is flawed is that the identification of a cohort is not straightforward. Schools may make an attempt to identify their gifted and talented children and instead create an inaccurate cohort. This not only causes difficulties for the cohort in question, in terms of expectations, etc., but also, and perhaps more importantly, can cut off opportunities for those not identified.

Definitions of what it means to be considered gifted and talented vary. Freeman (1998) defines the very able as: 'Those who demonstrate exceptionally high-level performance, whether across a range of endeavours or in a limited field, or those whose potential for excellence has not yet been recognised by either tests or experts.'

She also draws a useful distinction between the recognised gifts of children and those of adults. In the case of adults, recognition is based on products which are the result of many years of dedication in the chosen domain, whereas for children it is usually precociousness in comparison to others of a similar age. It is possible to observe precocious ability or behaviour in some activities in the primary school. However, not all abilities or talents show themselves in this way at an early age and even where they do, only a limited range can be accurately measured. For example, in some cases a facility with language may be obvious; a facility with history may be harder to pinpoint. Even where early precocious behaviour is observed, it is important to remember that it is only one indicator of giftedness.

For giftedness, as it is displayed by adults, research shows there are various developmental stages. Bloom and his colleagues (1985) looked at 120 young adults performing very highly in sport (swimming and tennis), fine arts (music and sculpture) and science (maths and neurology). They identified three general phases in their childhood development:

- the playful phase;
- the precision phase;
- the personal style phase.

The playful stage is characterised by a playful immersion in a field of interest. A child may find this activity rewarding and become interested in pursuing the field further, but this is largely a phase which involves enjoyment rather than striving for achievement. The second stage concerns the mastery of technical skills and a reaching for perfection. Here the child learns the 'rules of the game' and begins to master the techniques required for excellence in a given domain. The third, or personal phase, comes when a child is able to express their talent to create something new and uniquely different. In some activities or domains the personal stage does not come about for most gifted children until adolescence. Winner (1996) suggests that art may be an example of this where the move from the conventional phase to the post-conventional phase may not take place until well into adolescence. It is therefore difficult to identify at primary school age those who might excel in the third and crucial stage.

Gardner (2000) also suggests that the first and second phases can produce results which are confusing. The child in the playful phase encountering what Walters and Gardner (1986) call 'crystallising experiences' can, almost by chance, produce work which appears precocious. However, when they enter the second phase, precision or mastery, the ability to convert this into a more recognised and accepted form may not be demonstrated. Equally the mastery stage may itself produce outcomes that are so satisfying and rewarding for the child that they choose to remain at stage two and become technically proficient but not in any way original.

Yet another problem for the hapless primary school seeking to identify the gifted and talented is that giftedness is a complex phenomenon. As Zorman (1998) indicates:

It is not enough to measure specific abilities and talents. It is not even enough to measure the ability to learn when given mediation. Rather one must also search for the non-intellective components that may aid or deter development of talent and abilities.

What are these 'non-intellective components'? Jackson (2000) states that most current conceptualisations of giftedness in children stress the fortunate coincidence or interaction of multiple factors. These have been identified by various researchers as including motivation, personality, task commitment, opportunity, support from home, school and peers (Renzulli 1978, Monks 1992, Sternberg and Lubart 1992, Tannenbaum 1983, Feldman and Goldsmith 1996, and Gardner 1983).

Finally, there is the growing awareness that giftedness is multi-dimensional. It has long been recognised that children or adults may be gifted in a single area or in a range of domains. Gardner (1999) cites eight possible domains of intelligence, shown in Figure 1.3, in which an individual may display outstanding ability:

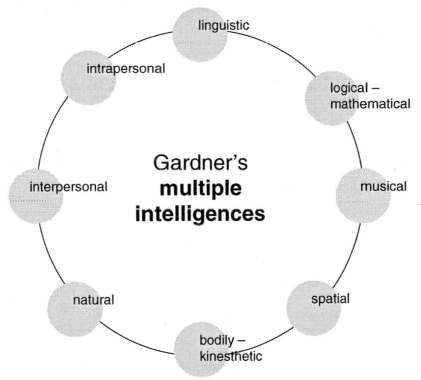

Figure 1.3 Gardner's multiple intelligences (Gardner 1999)

In his 'triarchic theory', Sternberg (1986) cites three areas:

- analytic intelligence;
- creative intelligence;
- practical intelligence.

What may be less familiar are findings from such researchers as Achter, Benbow and Lubinski (1997) and others, who have shown significant disparity between abilities in one domain and another. Differences in ability in language and maths were found to be the norm rather than the exception. Ninety-five per cent of the 1,000 gifted children they looked at had a considerable difference between their abilities in language and maths. As Winner (1996) puts it: 'Unevenness is the rule among academically gifted children while global gifted . . . is the exception'.

Implications of perspectives of giftedness

The most obvious conclusion from this review of the literature is that identification of gifted and talented in the primary school might at best be described as problematic and at worst as futile. Yet even when all these factors are taken into consideration it is obvious to any teacher that some of the pupils in his/her class are brighter than others and that curriculum opportunities need to be adjusted to take account of this.

So how might we begin to identify in primary school and what might be the purpose? We would suggest that the only purpose for attempting identification in primary school is to create a better match between the curriculum opportunities on offer and the child's cognitive needs; therefore it might be helpful to consider the following categories as children who have the potential to be gifted:

- children who appear to be exhibiting precocious talent or ability, i.e. they are achieving at a level significantly above that of their peers in one or a range of areas;
- particularly at Foundation Stage and Key Stage 1, children who are interested in an area and actively seek to pursue it, enjoying it for its own sake;
- children who appear to master the rules of a domain easily and can transfer their insights to new problems;
- children who observe their own behaviour and hence utilise a greater variety of learning strategies than others;
- children who exhibit any of the characteristics above plus a tendency towards non-conformity in the given domain.

Some of these categories can be measured, others cannot. It may be possible to create a register of gifted and talented children based on the first category but in doing so it is likely that some gifted children will be overlooked. The creation of a register is not in itself straightforward or even a universal good. Any school creating a register must recognise its limitations and avoid directing challenging opportunities only to the children on the register.

Key point

The universal dilemma for schools seeking to make effective provision for gifted and talented pupils is the need to provide well for the group of pupils already recognised as gifted or talented and at the same time create opportunities for those not yet recognised to display their ability. This leads us to conclude that effective identification will be a combination of the assessment of precocious achievement or behaviour plus an emphasis on creating the conditions which will allow giftedness to develop and reveal itself.

The following section considers the mechanisms for achieving both of those outcomes – a register of those with precocious abilities and school provision which allows others to reveal their developing abilities.

Methods for identifying precocious ability

The DfEE in its 'Excellence in Cities' initiative requires secondary schools to identify a cohort of pupils of between 5 per cent and 10 per cent of the overall school population who form the gifted and talented cohort and for whom a distinct teaching and learning programme should be available. This approach has been very successful in raising awareness of the needs of the gifted and talented and in encouraging curriculum experimentation. Even so the creation of the cohort has been the most problematic aspect of the policy and tensions have arisen in 'thinking' schools regarding the extent to which the cohort should consist primarily of those who already demonstrate high achievement or of those who may have potential to do so but currently do not achieve highly. In primary schools, for the reasons given above, this tension is magnified. In the secondary sector many pupils will have reached the third stage of development (personal originality) and providing that the curriculum is structured to value such original thought and ideas (and generally the National Curriculum and exam syllabuses are) then achievement should be the norm for most gifted pupils. Exceptions to this general rule come largely in relation to pupils who are underachieving for a variety of reasons.

In primary school, identification through high achievement is likely to account for significantly less of the 'gifted population' than in secondary schools, and therefore any register of gifted and talented pupils has to be regarded as significantly more speculative. In seeking to create such a register, three broad forms of information are available to schools. All these forms have strengths and weaknesses and therefore the use of a combination is thought by most researchers to be essential. Montgomery (1996) states: 'What is quite clear is that unidimensional methods and tests are not successful in identifying the able'.

Available information
1. Tests:

- baseline entry, SATs;
- cognitive ability or non-verbal reasoning tests;
- reading, spelling, maths;
- school progress and module tests.

2. Diagnostic assessment:

- based on the work children produce (portfolios);
- performance in class, especially in question/answer sessions;
- based on checklists of characteristics (general or subject specific).

3. Opinion:

- teacher nomination;
- parental nomination;
- self nomination;
- peer nomination.

The fashion for testing in school has increased in recent years as part of an overall approach to the use of data as a measure of school improvement. SATs and other forms of assessment undertaken by pupils at various stages in their school career can provide useful data to demonstrate that a child is achieving at a level in advance of their peers. Children achieving highly in SATs might reasonably be included in the gifted cohort although, as has already been mentioned, high achievement in SATs and baseline tends to focus on mastery of what Gardner (2000) calls the 'rules of the game' and therefore is a better indicator of a competent expert than of a potentially gifted adult.

Other forms of testing can also provide useful data, although they too have their limitations. The strengths and limitations of tests, and in particular IQ tests, are well covered in OFSTED's review of current international research (Freeman 1998). In fact Howe (1995) suggests that we will never find a test that can be administered in childhood that will reliably predict eventual adult achievement. Yet IQ tests are still used to identify the gifted. In 'Highly Able Children' (House of Commons 1999), evidence given as part of the inquiry into provision for the highly able suggested a discrepancy of view among experts as to the value of using tests as an indicator of ability. Evidence submitted to the inquiry suggested that parents find IQ tests useful in providing 'observable hard evidence' in discussing the issue with schools. (Perhaps this is an indicator that schools are not always as open minded as they could be when considering high ability.) Overall the inquiry found as follows:

> . . . the consensus of the evidence is that tests have some value in the recognition of both ability and achievement but are merely one form of evidence and cannot, in themselves, provide a definition of high ability.

Diagnostic assessment overcomes some of the problems related to tests and can help teachers to become better at recognising some aspects of high achievement. The English National Curriculum is helpful in assisting teachers to look up the 'levels' to decide how a piece of work might be judged and in providing a notional performance norm for pupils of a given age. Since the introduction of this type of national assessment framework, increasingly tighter judgements are being made on children's progress and this is obviously helpful in the identification of the gifted.

> Procedures for assessing pupils' attainment have continued to improve. (OFSTED 1999)

Portfolios provide one helpful way of collecting evidence of high levels of performance and can be particularly useful in recording the achievements of young children. These can consist of a variety of information collected over a period of time to demonstrate progress. Porter (1999) describes a portfolio as a 'systematic compilation of progress in all developmental domains and in particular in complex mental skills'. She includes a useful list from Wright and Borland (1993) outlining possible contents (see Figure 1.4).

Portfolios are particularly useful for charting the development of outstanding individuals or those whose talents are uneven. Portfolio-based evidence of achievement at a level significantly in advance of one's peers should be sufficient evidence for inclusion on a gifted register.

Checklists have proved a popular form of identification in schools but also have their problems. Few checklists are based on research evidence and many make use of anecdotal evidence so reducing their validity. In addition a checklist can only ever be a guide and give an overall sense of what it means to be gifted. Even experts disagree to some extent on the characteristics for inclusion. In the research-based checklist given below early symbolic activity is cited. This contrasts with the findings of Robinson, Dale and Landesman (in Robinson 2000) who suggest that young gifted children are not generally advanced in motor skills. Robinson indicates that the most reliable characteristics for young children are good memory, long attention span, extensive vocabulary, older playmates and personal maturity. Hence checklists must be viewed with caution. (Subject-specific checklists can be more helpful in identifying domain-specific ability as is demonstrated in later chapters of this book.)

Observational notes about children's language and behaviour which might signal their interests and thinking:

- typical examples or photographs of their work;
- notable examples of their work which might indicate their ability, potential or progress, particularly in their use of metacognitive skills;
- child-selected examples – preferably of pieces of work that are special to the children (rather than examples of their 'best' work). Included in these examples will be the children's reflections on the work, which they can dictate for you to write out;
- notable moment records, which can be small file cards on which you record illuminating occurrences that help to round out the picture of the child's skills;
- let-me-tell-you-about-my-child cards, which are the parents' contributions to the portfolio. Given that children can behave differently at home from in the early childhood setting, these cards add significantly to information about the child, involve parents in the early childhood programme and can help them focus on positive aspects of their child;
- finally, an exit summary report written by the caregiver or teacher on the basis of the contents of the portfolio.

Figure 1.4 A portfolio of evidence (Wright and Barland 1993)

The most reliable forms of checklist are those based on actual research. The checklist below is based on the outcomes of work by Shore in which he was exploring the ways in which gifted children think (Freeman 1998, adapted from Shore 1991):

- memory and knowledge – excellent memory and use of information;
- self-regulation – they know how they learn best and can monitor their learning;
- speed of thought – they may spend longer on planning but then reach decisions more speedily;
- dealing with problems – they add to information, spot what is irrelevant and get to the essentials more quickly;
- flexibility – although their thinking is usually more organised than other children's, they can see and adopt alternative solutions to learning and problem solving;
- preference for complexity – they tend to make games and tasks more complex to increase interest;
- concentration – they have an exceptional ability to concentrate at will and for long periods of time from an early age;
- early symbolic ability – they may speak, read and write very early.

Finally, the category of opinion. The younger the child the more likely that identification will rely on observation of behaviour. Parents are likely to be effective in identification since they observe their children most frequently. Robinson (2000) in her study of 100 kindergartners found that the responses of parents clearly correlated with their children's assessed behaviour. Of course, such identification is reliant on an understanding of the indicators of ability, and therefore parents in American studies are often given checklists of characteristics to help them in their assessment. Much work has been done to consider the effectiveness of teachers in identifying gifted and talented pupils. Once again the research base for this is well covered in Freeman (1998). The overall finding is that teachers can be effective in identifying the gifted and talented provided they have been trained in what to look for. Without training they tend to confuse ability with neat, tidy, conforming children. Our view would be that teacher identification is an essential part of the on-going identification process but that untrained teacher assessment can be inaccurate and dangerous.

Key point

Teachers in primary school should see themselves as 'talent spotters', constantly on the lookout for signs of ability or talent.

Methods for revealing ability

If revelation of ability is to be a partner to the more formal identification of precocious ability, it must in its own way be rigorous and systematic. There are three key areas for schools to consider in this area if they are to ensure effectiveness in identification through provision.

a) **Providing the context**

Here a school has two responsibilities: it must ensure range of provision and quality of provision. Range is important because it allows children to discover their talents. A child never introduced to improvised drama is unlikely to know that they have a talent for this. Many adults discover new abilities and talents in later life and this will always be the case. It is not possible for schools to offer opportunities in every talent area but this is a strong argument for a broad and balanced curriculum. This also applies to children who demonstrate precocious ability in a particular domain. While they may wish to pursue their initial domain of interest it is important to continue the process of offering opportunities in new areas because they may find they have additional domains of talent. Just because a child is good at maths it does not mean they should be excused art, they may discover they are equally talented in this area.

The quality of what is offered is equally as important as the range. If schools have low expectations of their children and set tasks accordingly then it is difficult for those with the ability to achieve highly. Equally, if challenging opportunities are always offered to a restricted group then those outside the group are unable to demonstrate high levels of achievement. Where challenging opportunities are a regular feature of classroom provision then children will demonstrate their abilities through high level responses.

b) **Observation of emerging ability**

For identification through provision to occur it is necessary for outstanding outcomes to be observed. These outcomes might be in the form of written work, practical work or class discussion and debate. Two forms of observation should operate in the effective school. First, the teacher should be involved in an on-going process of talent spotting. She or he may keep a log of significant responses or comments and these placed together form a body of identification evidence. Second, systematic observation may take place from time to time with another adult observing the pupil's responses while the teacher teaches. This second option allows for close observation which is difficult for the teacher to achieve when teaching the lesson.

c) **Recording of outcomes**

As part of the regular process of updating the gifted and talented register, outcomes from the 'identification through provision' process should be collected and submitted. In this way new talents will be uncovered and children added to the list. An effective school is likely to revisit its identification framework at least annually, although of course individual teachers will adjust their cognitive demands on individual children as soon as significant ability is demonstrated.

Key point

For a school to provide high-quality identification procedures, its framework must include both methods for recognising precocious ability and for revealing emergent ability.

Modifying the curriculum to create challenge

The fundamental question facing schools when looking to improve provision for gifted and talented pupils is as follows: What do we need to change in our existing curriculum in order to make it sufficiently challenging and motivating for gifted and talented children? This question has a uniquely English context and must be addressed accordingly. The National Curriculum outlines in considerable detail the knowledge, skills and concepts to be taught and even links them to specific recommended ages. This is quite different from other countries, for example USA and Australia.

The National Curriculum

Much of the influential international literature on curriculum planning, e.g. Van Tassel-Baska (1992) and Maker and Nielson (1995), focuses on creating a curriculum which meets the needs of the gifted and talented. Here in England we are not actually creating a curriculum but rather assessing the effectiveness of our existing, nationally determined, curriculum and making necessary adjustments or modifications to it. This has both advantages and disadvantages. The most significant disadvantage is highlighted by Montgomery (2000): 'We now have the situation where the National Curriculum and the methods by which it is taught have especially not led to a stimulating and educative experience for the gifted and talented'.

A preoccupation with content coverage and skills acquisition has led some teachers to focus on delivery rather than learning: what is being taught, rather than how it is being taught and what is being learnt. At worst this has actually reduced access to the kinds of learning opportunities most appropriate for gifted children.

The advantages of having a National Curriculum surround the possibilities of exploiting its requirements in an imaginative way. The National Curriculum is not in itself prescriptive as regards teaching methodologies and does include opportunities for higher order thinking – indeed it actively encourages children to 'use and apply' knowledge in Science and Maths. While some teachers have become focused on didactic content delivery, others have used the same curriculum requirements to create challenging, stimulating and imaginative lessons. Even where teaching methodologies have been centrally prescribed in England, i.e. the literacy and numeracy strategies, some teachers have used the approaches to challenge their gifted pupils.

Key point

The National Curriculum can provide an effective context for exploring possibilities for using particular theoretical models or approaches.

Teachers in the Bristol 'Flying High' project (Bristol LEA 2001) successfully used Bloom's taxonomy as the basis for creating challenge in their literacy and numeracy work and in one school all planning documents were assessed to ascertain the incidence of tasks requiring higher order thinking, as a method of increasing the incidence of higher level activity in short-term planning (see Appendix One).

How might a curriculum be changed?

Researchers looking to improve provision for gifted pupils are generally looking to provide a curriculum which is what Maker and Nielson (1995) call 'qualitatively different from the programme for all students'. Gallagher (1985) suggested that changes could be made to the content, method and learning environment. Figure 1.5 is adapted from Maker and Nielson (1995) and outlines the various possibilities available.

In practice the range of possibilities can be bewildering and most teachers seeking to improve their practice begin by selecting a small range of approaches and deploying them where possible.

Changes to content (including process and product):
- enrichment – variety;
- extension – complexity/abstractness;
- higher order thinking – analysis, synthesis, evaluation;
- enquiry/problem solving;
- scaffolded learning (Vygotsky 1978);
- social interactional approaches.

Changes to method:
- task modification;
- questioning;
- increased pace;
- increased independence;
- increased direction;
- intellectual risk taking.

Changes to the learning context:
- programmes for the gifted;
- withdrawal groups;
- selective classes;
- mixed ability classrooms (differentiation);
- classes with older children (acceleration);
- non-school contexts.

Figure 1.5 Curriculum changes (Adapted from Maker and Nielson 1995)

Changing the curriculum for selected gifted pupils or changing it for all?

When Maker and Nielson refer to creating a programme for the gifted that is 'qualitatively different' from the programme for all students they make an assumption that such a curriculum would only be suitable for the gifted. This perspective has dominated the work on gifted and talented in the USA and Australia and led to the creation of special programmes for the gifted. The question of whether these 'qualitatively different' aspects of curriculum provision are useful for all children is only beginning to be explored in the USA and Canada (Shore 2000). In England it has been more thoroughly explored, although comprehensive empirical research studies of any scale are still lacking.

Teacher-researchers looking to develop their classroom practice in England have largely focused on in-class programmes, therefore, a body of small scale work now exists spanning approximately 20 years. Two interesting findings have emerged from this work. First, it is possible for teachers to adjust their regular planning to provide work which meets the 'qualitatively different' requirement of Maker and Nielson and to provide this as part of the ordinary classroom offer (Eyre and Marjoram 1990, Eyre and Fuller 1993). Second, where teachers have focused on planning to create challenge for the most able/gifted pupils, they often then choose to make the task available to a wider group of children, sometimes offering additional support to allow other pupils to access the same task. Reasons given for this by teachers in the Oxfordshire Primary Teacher Research Network are both pragmatic and pedagogical. In terms of classroom management a reduction in the number of tasks on offer allows for smoother operation and time for the teacher to work with individuals. In pedagogical terms the challenging tasks require more 'expert behaviour' or 'higher order thinking' and lead to higher levels of attainment but are also intellectually stimulating and likely to be highly motivating regardless of a child's ability level.

The significance of these findings should not be underestimated. They provide compelling evidence of the benefits of an inclusive approach to the education of the gifted as advocated in Eyre (1997), Freeman (1998) and Montgomery (1996 and 2000). This kind of approach also goes some way towards solving the problems created by difficulties in the identification of young gifted children. If the 'qualitatively different' curriculum is a regular feature of general classroom provision, then those who can demonstrate 'gifted behaviour' should reveal themselves. In 1992 Her Majesty's Inspectorate (HMI) found that where specific attention was paid to the needs of gifted children there was often a general increase in the level of expectation of all children. This is likely to be as a result of teachers adopting an inclusive view of provision.

Of course, not all challenging opportunities can be made available in this way. Sometimes a task is only suitable for the small group of children in the class who can demonstrate particular skills (e.g. working with very complex text) and therefore flexible ability grouping does have a significant place in effective curriculum provision. Equally, as Shore (2000) points out, the stimulation provided by intellectual peers aids cognitive development and therefore gifted or talented children need a chance to work with others of like ability. This may mean some access to extra activities for those gifted in a particular area (enrichment opportunities).

What do we mean by a challenge

Much is said about the need to create more challenging opportunities for gifted and talented children. These can be created by any of the methods above but what do we actually mean when we describe something as challenging? Hertzog, Klein and Katz (1999), in a paper on challenging young gifted children, describe it as follows: 'A challenging activity would be one that would cause the students to perform at a level that extends beyond their comfort zone'.

Vygotsky (1978) introduced to education the idea of the zone of proximal development:

> The difference between the actual developmental level as determined by independent problem solving, and the level of potential development as determined through problem solving under adult guidance or in collaboration with more capable peers.

Both Vygotsky and Hertzog *et al.* indicate that in order for an activity to be challenging it must require the individual to strive for success rather than achieve it effortlessly. For gifted children many requirements of the school curriculum, deemed appropriate for children of their age, can be achieved effortlessly and are not challenging. Modification of the curriculum for gifted children should seek to increase challenge through the introduction of higher level thinking, skills development and problem solving. It is worth noting at this point that much 'so called' extension work provided in schools does not meet this criterion. Rather it focuses on increasing the volume of work undertaken by gifted pupils, often meaning more work at the same level.

The Vygotsky zone of proximal development does not just focus on increased levels of difficulty but also recognises that work which is overdemanding may prove impossible and demotivating. This is the same for gifted children as for those who find learning difficult. Hence effective assessment of children's current levels of understanding is absolutely crucial to creating effective challenge. Csikszentmihalyi (1990) uses the term 'flow', to describe a state of mind in which suitable challenge is linked to appropriate skills. To achieve a state of 'flow' expectations must be high enough to require an individual to strive while skills levels must be good enough to allow for the goal to be achieved. Where expectation is too high and skills too low frustration is the result; where expectation is too low and skills too high, boredom (see Figure 1.6).

high challenge low skill	low challenge low skill
high challenge high skill	low challenge high skill

Mihaly Csikszentmihalyi (1990)

Figure 1.6 Flow

Each individual has a different set of circumstances in which she or he encounters flow. Some individuals can cope with more challenge than others; some find risk taking exhilarating, others find it frightening. Modifications to the school curriculum for gifted children should aim for flow, not for pressure. Too much low level activity does not lead to flow and too much acceleration of learning can lead to pressure. Learning should be fun and, if the development of ability or talent loses that element of fun, then we are unlikely to produce rounded, fulfilled individuals. This is especially important in the early years where skills levels and cognitive ability are often not well matched. It is worth remembering that some of the best mathematicians have found learning their tables by rote to be an impossible task. This does not make learning tables a pointless activity, but it is a reminder that those who show high levels of competence in low level tasks are not necessarily the most able.

How gifted children think and learn

If the aim of a primary school is to adjust or modify its curriculum provision to make it more appropriate for gifted and talented pupils, then an understanding of how gifted pupils think and learn is essential.

Gilhooley (1996) describes thinking thus:

> Thinking is an activity that has long intrigued and puzzled psychologists and philosophers – and continues to do so. Since all valuable innovations in the arts and sciences originate from fruitful thinking, it is a process of evident importance. At a more prosaic level, thought is frequently required to deal with various frustrations that arise in everyday activities. Even when not dealing with any pressing problems, thinking is always occurring, during periods of wakefulness, albeit often in a free flowing daydreaming fashion.

In recent years, in England, growing attention has been given to the importance of developing children's thinking. Fisher (1992) has led the way in primary schools with his work on teaching thinking, and Shayer and Adey's (1981) pioneering work on using cognitive conflict in science (CASE) has been highly influential in secondary schools. McGuinness (1999) provided a review of current research into thinking skills and related areas for the DfEE. She concluded, perhaps not surprisingly, that successful approaches tend to have a strong theoretical underpinning, well-designed and contextualised materials, explicit pedagogy and good teacher support. What must concern the primary school looking at creating effective provision for gifted and talented children is whether a general increase in a focus on thinking will in itself improve provision for gifted children.

Bruce Shore and his team at McGill University in Montreal have been exploring the thinking and learning of gifted children for many years and conclude that gifted learners do seem to use strategies that others never use (Shore 2000). These strategies include a three-way interaction between speed, flexibility and metacognitive knowledge. Shore found that gifted pupils could usually work with both speed and accuracy but that **accuracy** was the salient characteristic in high ability. Most gifted pupils who are prone to make careless errors learn to concentrate on accuracy because **self monitoring** is one of the strategies they invoke frequently. The ability to reflect on our thinking processes (**metacognition**) is seen by Shore as linked to both flexible thinking and to high ability. Some gifted children were found to be flexible thinkers while others were less so, but all gifted children were aware of the need to explore alternative solutions when obvious ones failed to work. What is interesting here is that gifted children are using the approaches which are recognised as those used by adults expert in their field. They may not be producing outstanding results but they are using the same strategies. Shore suggests that gifted children draw on a repertoire of skills that are available to others but use them more imaginatively and self monitor or regulate their use to produce outcomes of increasing sophistication.

This would suggest that for a school to provide effectively for its gifted and talented children a focus on the development of critical and creative thinking linked to metacognition would provide a good basis for the approach. This is in itself not a new or original idea. Most of the recent literature in this field in England (Montgomery 1996, Eyre 1997, Koshy and Casey 1998, Freeman 1998) reaches this conclusion. What is more interesting is to examine the extent to which the thinking skills approach, which is being widely advocated for all children, can provide the basis for gifted and talented provision. In essence a focus on the development of thinking will lead, in part, to the use of problem solving, problem creating and higher order thinking. It will also promote self regulation of ideas and metacognition. This approach, if well handled by the teacher, can prompt gifted pupils to invoke creative or innovative solutions and begin to produce unique or original ideas. However, even when thinking skills approaches are used to provide challenge for the gifted, suitable learning goals need to be identified.

Key point

Well-grounded approaches which focus on developing thinking are good for all children, however, appropriately used, they can also provide a vehicle for the deployment of the complex repertoire of intellectual skills manifested by gifted children.

A second issue related to the learning of gifted and talented pupils concerns differences in learning styles between the precociously talented child and the potentially gifted adult. If all giftedness were related to precocious ability then an appropriate educational response might be to allow children to progress rapidly through the curriculum in order to succeed early and move on further than others, but the research evidence suggests that achievement is not merely a race, with the gifted being the faster runners. Giftedness or expertise is the result of efficient learning and a good deal of hard work and practice. Howe (1995) says:

Exceptional people climb higher than the rest of us do, though they may climb faster and more efficiently. But they do climb all the same, just like everyone else. No one miraculously arrives at the peak of their accomplishments.

So all children, including the gifted, need to learn to concentrate and persevere, even when outcomes are unrewarding. Even gifted children need to learn the 'rules of the game'. They need to learn the techniques required to play the piano or the skills needed to make a good football player. They need to learn how to create a beginning and an end to a piece of writing and how to calculate quickly in mental maths. They will tend to learn these skills efficiently and progress rapidly in skills acquisition, and so they will need either to move on to learning new skills before their peers or to begin to use and apply the skills learnt with increasing rigour. If a child has learnt a skill more quickly than others then two options are available. First, the child can move on to a new skill, or second, they can 'apply' that skill. If a child is introduced with his/her peers to the techniques for beginning stories, they can continue to apply and develop this skill indefinitely by looking at less conventional approaches, the way particular writers use openings, the use of beginnings in different centuries etc. This coupled with an emphasis on self monitoring of work produced should assist the child to produce innovative and imaginative approaches to the problem of how to create an effective beginning. In the literature this is defined as **extension** (Eyre and Marjoram 1990) and can provide a viable alternative to moving on to the next concept (**acceleration**).

An effective classroom for gifted and talented

This book is concerned to offer practical ideas on how to make effective classroom provision for the gifted and talented in the core curriculum areas. This section, therefore, has restricted itself to looking at cross-curricular or generic approaches and to considering measures of effectiveness. Determining what might constitute effectiveness in classroom provision is a key consideration for any school. This chapter has looked at the range of issues that might be taken into account and how these might influence school and provision. The following checklist (Figure 1.7) is based on a synthesis of the research findings mentioned at earlier points in this chapter and presents an overall framework for reviewing classroom provision.

For teachers reviewing their own practice or that of others there is a need for a more detailed set of indicators which are linked to existing practice in the school. Figure 1.8 takes the points made in Figure 1.7 and expands them to provide a framework for staff discussion and also for possible monitoring. Each of the points in Figure 1.8 provides a stimulus for staffroom discussion and could usefully form an agenda for school improvement in the education of gifted and talented pupils. Why, for example, is it necessary to have a combination of subject expertise and teacher enthusiasm? One answer may be that while subject expertise is vital in recognising the progression routes within the subject and the potential for

---

Effective classroom provision for gifted and talented pupils:

1. builds on what we know about how gifted and talented children think and learn;
2. offers opportunities to reveal ability as well as operate at high levels;
3. offers structured access to higher levels of achievement;
4. uses assessment for determining learning as well as assessing learning outcomes;
4. requires children to strive, persist and self regulate;
5. makes learning enjoyable as well as challenging and rewards intellectual risk taking and innovation.

Figure 1.7 Effective classroom provision

Classroom considerations

- Agreement regarding higher level skills children might acquire within the subject
- High teacher expectation
- Subject expertise and teacher enthusiasm
- Variety in teaching styles and nature of tasks
- Teacher-pupil relationship which encourages questions, personal reflection and the formulation of personal opinions
- Clear outcomes both generally and for most able
- Balance between structure and independence
- Recognition of prior learning
- Honest feedback and target setting
- Assessment which relates to objectives and does over measure
- Interest in teaching and learning the subject, not just the syllabus
- Fun and laughter and maybe a little quirkiness
- No artificial ceilings
- No MOTS (more of the same) or overload

Figure 1.8 A framework for discussion

challenge within tasks it does not in itself motivate children. Gifted and talented children are motivated by both knowledge and fun (Joswig 1998) and therefore an effective teacher of gifted and talented children will provide both.

For the classroom teacher seeking to create effective challenge, a wide variety of approaches are available which can help to deliver the curriculum in such a way as to offer opportunities that capitalise on the way gifted and talented children think and learn. Some approaches are best suited to particular subjects but others have a more universal appeal. Figure 1.9 is adapted from a more detailed section on classroom planning in Eyre (1997) and considers some of the available approaches that might usefully provide a menu for the busy teacher.

---

20 Ideas for Creating Challenge

- Plan / Do / Review
- Work from difficult text
- Use a range of information
- Recording in an unusual way
- Role play
- Problem solving and enquiry tasks
- Choice in how to handle content
- Decision making
- No correct answer
- Provide answer, they set questions
- Work from one text or artefact
- Involving pupils in the planning
- Time restricted activities
- Developing metacognition
- Bloom's higher order thinking
- Study skills, using D.A.R.T.S.
- Employing technical language
- Modelling experts
- Philosophy
- Book Talk (Aidan Chambers)

Figure 1.9 Creating Challenge

References

Achter, J. A., Benbow, C. P. and Lubinski, D. (1997) 'Rethinking multipotentiality among the intellectually gifted: A critical review and recommendations', *Gifted Child Quarterly* **41**, 5–15.

Bloom, B. (ed.) (1985) *Developing Talent in Young People*. New York: Basic Books.

Bristol LEA (2001) *Flying High in Bristol*. Bristol: Bristol LEA.

Clark, C. and Callow, F. (1998) *Educating Able Children*. London: David Fulton Publishers.

Csikszentmihalyi, M. (1990) *Flow: The Psychology of Optimal Experience*. New York: Harper and Row.

DfEE (1999) *Excellence in Cities*. London: HMSO.

Eyre, D. (1997) *Able Children in Ordinary Schools*. London: David Fulton Publishers.

Eyre, D. (1999) 'Ten years of provision for the gifted in Oxfordshire ordinary schools: insights into policy and practice', *Gifted and Talented International* **14**, 12–20.

Eyre, D. and Marjoram, T. (1990) *Enriching and Extending the National Curriculum*. London: Kogan Page.

Eyre, D. and Fuller, M. (1993) *Year 6 Teachers and More Able Children*. Oxford: National Primary Centre.

Feldman, D. H. (with Goldsmith, L.) (1996) *Nature's Gambit: Child Prodigies and the Development of Human Potential.* New York: Basic Books.

Fisher, R. (1992) *Teaching Children to Think.* Cheltenham: Stanley Thornes (Publishers) Ltd.

Freeman, J. (1998) *Educating the Very Able: Current International Research.* London: HMSO.

Gallagher, J. J. (1985) *Teaching the Gifted Child.* Newton: Allyn and Bacon Inc.

Gardner, H. (1983) *Frames of Mind: The Theory of Multiple Intelligences.* New York: Basic Books.

Gardner, H. (1999) *Intelligence Reframed: Multiple Intelligences for the 21st Century.* New York: Basic Books.

Gardner, H. (2000) 'The giftedness matrix: a developmental perspective', in Friedman, R. C. and Shore, B. M. (eds) *Talents Unfolding: Cognition and Development.* Washington DC: American Psychological Association.

Gilhooley, K. J. (1996) *Thinking: Directed, Undirected and Creative.* London: Academic Press.

Hertzog, N. B., Klein, M. M. and Katz L. G. (1999) 'Hypothesising and theorising: challenge in an early childhood curriculum', *Gifted and Talented International,* 14, 38–49.

HMI (1992) *Education Observed: The Education of Very Able Children in Maintained Schools.* London: HMSO.

House of Commons (1999) Education and Employment Committee, Third Report, 'Highly Able Children'. London: HMSO.

Howe, M. (1995) 'What can we learn from the lives of geniuses?', in Freeman, J. (ed.) *Actualizing Talent.* London: Cassell.

Ireson, J. and Hallam, S. (1999) 'Raising standards: is ability grouping the answer', *Oxford Review of Education,* 25(3), 343–58.

Jackson, N. E. (2000) 'Strategies for modeling the development of giftedness in children', in Friedman, R. C. and Shore, B. M. (eds) *Talents Unfolding: Cognition and Development.* Washington DC: American Psychological Association.

Joswig, H. (1998) 'Motivational learning conditions in gifted pupils', *Gifted and Talented International,* 13, 28–33.

Kennard, R. (1996) *Teaching Mathematically Able Children.* Oxford: NACE (National Association for Able Children in Education).

Kerry, T. and Kerry, C. (2000) 'The centrality of teaching skills in improving able pupil education', *Educating Able Children,* 4(2), 13–19.

Koshy, V. and Casey, R. (1998) *Effective Provision for Able and Exceptionally Able Children.* London: Hodder and Stoughton.

Lee-Corbin, H. and Denicolo, P. (1998) *Able Children in Primary Schools.* London: David Fulton Publishers.

McGuinness, C. (1999) *From thinking skills to thinking classrooms.* DfEE research brief no.115. London: DfEE.

Maker, C. J. and Nielson, A. B. (1995) *Teaching Models in Education of the Gifted.* Texas: pro-ed.

Monks, F. J. (1992) 'Development of gifted children: the issues of identification and programming', in Monks, F. J. and Peters, W. (eds) *Talent for the Future.* Assen/Maastricht: Van Gorcum.

Montgomery, D. (1996) *Educating the Able.* London: Cassell.

Montgomery, D. (2000) 'Inclusive education for able underachievers: changing teaching and learning', in Montgomery, D. (ed.) *Able Underachievers.* London: Whurr.

OFSTED (1999) *Annual Report of Chief Inspector for Schools 1998/99.* London: The Stationery Office.

Porter, L. (1999) *Gifted Young Children.* Buckingham: Open University Press.

Renzulli, J. S. (1978) 'What makes giftedness? Reexamining a definition', *Phi Delta Kappan*, **60**, 180–84.

Robinson, N. M. (2000) 'Giftedness in very young children: how seriously should it be taken?', in Friedman, R. C. and Shore, B. M. (eds) *Talents Unfolding: Cognition and Development.* Washington DC: American Psychological Association.

Sammons, P., Hillman, J. and Mortimore, P. (1996) *Key Characteristics of Effective Schools.* Ringwood: MBC Distribution Services.

Shayer, M. and Adey, P. (1981) *Towards a Science of Science Teaching.* Oxford: Heinemann.

Shore, B. M. (1991) 'How do gifted children think differently?', *AGATE (Journal of the Gifted and Talented Education Council of Alberta Teachers Association)* 5(2), 19–23.

Shore, B. M. (2000) 'Metacognition and flexibility: qualitative differences in how gifted children think', in Friedman, R. C. and Shore, B. M. (eds) *Talents Unfolding: Cognition and Development.* Washington DC: American Psychological Association.

Sternberg, R. J. (1986) 'A triarchic theory of intelligence', in Sternberg, R. J. and Davidson, J. E. (eds) *Conceptions of Giftedness.* Cambridge: Cambridge University Press.

Sternberg, R. J. and Lubart, T. I. (1992) 'Creative giftedness', in Colangelo, N., Assouline, S. G. and Ambroson, D. L. (eds) *Talent Development: Proceedings from the 1991 Henry B. and Jocelyn Wallace National Research Symposium on Talent Development* (66–88). Unionville, New York: Trillium.

Stopper, M. J. (2000) *Meeting the Social and Emotional Needs of Gifted and Talented Children.* London: David Fulton Publishers.

Tannenbaum, A. J. (1983) *Gifted children: psychological and educational perspectives.* New York: Macmillan

Van Tassel-Baska, J. (1992) *Planning Effective Curriculum for Gifted Learners.* Denver, Colorado: Love Publishing Company.

Vygotsky, L. S. (1978) *Mind in Society.* Cambridge Mass: Harvard University Press.

Walters, J. and Gardner, H. (1986) 'Crystallizing experience', in Sternberg, R. J. and Davidson, J. E. (eds), *Conceptions of Giftedness.* New York: Cambridge University Press.

Winner, E. (1996) *Gifted Children: Myths and Realities.* New York: Basic Books.

Wright, L. and Borland, J. H. (1993) 'Using early childhood developmental portfolios in the identification and education of young, economically disadvantaged, potentially gifted students', *Roeper Review,* 15(4), 205–10.

Zorman, R. (1998) 'A model for adolescent giftedness identification via challenges (MAGIC)', *Gifted and Talented International,* 13, 65–72.

CHAPTER 2
English

Jackie Holderness

Introduction

> Primary and secondary schools do not usually make the best sort of provision for pupils with more advanced linguistic and language abilities, because they are not looking out for them. They do not anticipate their arrival and do not notice their presence. Many schools also fail to have in place the necessary language enhancing curriculum which would allow these pupils to thrive. (Dean 1998, p. 8)

This chapter considers what teachers may do to improve provision for able language users. It looks briefly at the current contexts for the teaching of English and then explores approaches to the anticipation, identification, assessment and evaluation of the gifted in English. Next, it examines the 'language enhancing' curriculum. This includes organisational issues and ways to plan and enhance provision, with examples of extension and enrichment opportunities, taken from Key Stages 1 and 2. Finally, it considers opportunities beyond the classroom and the value of good home-school partnerships, for it is in the home that giftedness in language is likely to first become obvious.

Language development in able children

It has been shown (Wells 1987, Brice-Heath 1983) that the quality and nature of adult-child interaction in the preschool years can significantly affect a child's language use and academic performance in school. Fowler (in Howe 1990) in a study of gifted language user research, decided that intensive early verbal stimulation helped to develop excellence in language and logic, but noted that 'Learning to use language, to learn letters and to read were not viewed by parents (of gifted children) as ends in themselves but as doors opening opportunities to gain knowledge, academic competence or literary excellence, all of which were variously stressed from the beginning' (p. 196).

What seems to be a significant factor in language success, in any culture, is being accepted as a maker of meaning. Caregivers ascribe meaning to the language and behaviour of young children, often remodelling toddler talk into fuller, syntactically accurate utterances. For example, the child says, 'Ball, ball' and the parent responds 'Ah, you want the rugby ball do you? No? Maybe this red and yellow ball? Yes? Here it is'. Bruner (1986) refers to this kind of extension and support as 'scaffolding'.

Able children who demonstrate sophisticated vocabulary and high levels of oral fluency have usually had positive and extended exchanges with their caregivers. They have been encouraged to ask questions and articulate their ideas. A certain degree of metalinguistic awareness is likely have been encouraged by caregivers pointing out oral and written word patterns, discussing word origins and variations in usage, e.g. 'Isn't it funny how all these TRI- words have something to do with the number three? Can you think of any other words with TRI-? Ah, tricycle! How many wheels has a tricycle got? Yes, three! Just like a TRI-angle has three sides and three corners'. Many able children demonstrate an early ability to 'play' with words, creating verbal jokes, puns and nonsense languages of their own (see Figure 2.1).

A six year old child, combining his predeliction for making up jokes and puns and his fascination with long words, asked his parents:
   'What is a fortune teller's favourite word?'
   When they admitted defeat, he triumphantly announced that it was:
'SUPERCALIFRAGI – MYSTIC – EXPIALLYDOCIOUS!'
   He then wrote his invented word, with only two spelling mistakes and then defined mystic as 'a magical way to look into the future and see what's coming. . .' because he was not convinced his parents would understand the joke.

Figure 2.1 Punning and playing with Language (Year 1)

The value of such wordplay, rhymes, jingles and songs and their links with future reading potential has been established by Goswami and Bryant (1990). Familiarity with nursery rhymes, for example, indicates later success in learning to read. Once able language users start school, they may already be well on the road to literacy. They may enter school as fluent readers working towards Levels 2 or 3 of the National Curriculum.

The introduction of baseline assessment has meant, in principle, that it is possible to identify children with exceptional abilities in language on or soon after entry. It then becomes the school's responsibility to ensure that children continue to build upon their prior knowledge and language experience and develop their full potential in English.

Identifying able language users

There are several lists of criteria to help teachers identify able children (Wallace 2000; Eyre 1997). For a subject specific list, for English, the one devised by Evans and Goodhew (1997 p. 20) is useful:

A child who is gifted in language:

- demonstrates a high level of technical correctness;
- writes complex sentences using extensive vocabulary;
- is able to write and speak in a variety of registers and styles to suit audience;
- achieves excellence in creative writing;
- can identify and demonstrate irony, humour, absurdity, implied meaning;
- experiments with plot and character; displays originality;
- demonstrates speed and depth of understanding in the spoken and written word;
- is able to express and debate ideas in discussion;
- displays enthusiasm for the subject;
- is able to select, extract and synthesise facts from a passage of writing;
- is a sustained reader of a wide range of materials.

It is important that teachers move on from identification to planning for provision and to the establishment of assessment procedures to ensure that able language users who are slow developers are identified. Teachers need also to make sure that they are making progress commensurate with their ability and are not 'coasting' in English until the rest of the class 'catch up'.

Identifying underachievers in English

A problem for many able language users concerns the activities they are asked to do in school. Where tasks are unchallenging or emphasise convergent rather than divergent thinking, they may not inspire commitment and may limit creativity. Underachievers may therefore appear frustrated or exhibit challenging behaviours. Some children who are articulate and mature at home will hide their abilities by talking in a disguised, even babyish voice, and by using immature vocabulary. Several encounter social difficulties because their vocabulary and even their interests make them seem different from their peers. They may become withdrawn and isolated.

Lee-Corbin and Denicolo (1998) found in their study which explored significant factors associated with achievement: 'difficulties in (hand) writing can disadvantage pupils who would otherwise be considered able. Teachers may sometimes judge good performance in language on the neatness of presentation' (p. 52).

Where an articulate and able reader who should be capable of high levels of achievement is underperforming, there may be a learning difficulty such as dyslexia, a problem with motor control, e.g. pencil hold or an emotional block against writing, as in Figure 2.2.

Identifying able pupils who are EAL

A pupil whose mother tongue is not English may be an able language user but, unless the teacher speaks the same language as the child, he or she may not recognise the child's potential. Where possible, a bilingual support teacher or the parents can identify and record exceptional ability in language. Because of their abilities, the EAL child is likely to make excellent progress in English, provided that

An able reader was underachieving in written work across the curriculum. His teacher realised the problem related to the boy's pencil grip and the degree of pressure he exerted on his pencil. There was a 'writer's block' but she thought this was a defence mechanism the boy had devised to cover up his own awareness of the widening gulf between his cognitive abilities and his academic work. Together with the boy's parents, a handwriting 'campaign' was agreed. The boy was asked to write more and more softly and to write daily for ten minutes without stopping, copying or composing anything he wished. The goals were to:

a) press more lightly;
b) write more lines in the time allowed;
c) write in a flowing style, joining where appropriate.

By the following term, there was improvement in all three target areas and the boy went on to become an enthusiastic writer in all subjects.

Figure 2.2 An understanding writer (Year 4)

there is planned support and provision and the child is not left simply to learn vocabulary and structures as if 'by osmosis' in the playground and classroom.

The context: the National Curriculum, Curriculum 2000 and the National Literacy Strategy

The National Curriculum for English

In many ways, the National Curriculum may have enhanced opportunities for able children by providing a map, for teachers and parents, which outlines a pathway of progression across the key stages. Unfortunately, while primary teachers often succeed in providing challenge by extending and enriching the programmes of study and by employing various strategies to increase challenge (Eyre 1997) able language users may find, on arrival at secondary school, that there is little differentiation in their English lessons or homework, other than by outcome (Dean 1998).

Montgomery (1996) warns that the sheer volume and the content-based nature of the National Curriculum means that 'it is still unlikely that there will be sufficient time for able pupils to work at an appropriate level' (p. 63). She points out that there is still too little space for a process-based approach where 'Learners' interests and needs determine the direction of study in key content areas, and learners construct knowledge themselves'. (p. 64)

The National Literacy Strategy

The National Literacy Strategy may have helped able pupils in English because of:

- its provision of clear teaching objectives and INSET and teaching materials;
- its emphasis on differentiation through setting and ability grouping, through guided reading and guided writing;
- its breath, with access to a significantly wider range of texts and a greater focus on non-narrative forms;

- its provision of enhanced opportunities for pupils to work at their own pace.

One of the difficulties related to the introduction of the numeracy and literacy hours is the extensive demands they make on teachers' time. There is a distinct possibility that the broad curriculum is being 'squeezed' into the afternoon and some literacy activities, such as sustained writing are being restricted. The NLS Handbook, however, reassures teachers that there is flexibility within the literacy hour, especially for groups with specific needs:

> The Literacy Hour could be extended for some days, but not for all, in a week to provide focused sessions for particular groups, e.g. summer entrants in the reception year, **able children**, low attainers, children who need help to prepare for or follow up class work' (p. 9).

With regard to shared reading and writing sessions, the National Literacy Strategy (NLS) Handbook (1999) claims that 'Whole class work also benefits more able pupils'. and describes how successful teachers tailor questions and invite contributions to increase and vary the levels of challenge. In the process, teachers are encouraging able children, 'to explain and justify their ideas, to make generalisations, generate hypotheses, and offer critical comments' (p. 96).

With the NLS teaching objectives, teachers of able pupils need to be flexible and devise strategies to enhance the language curriculum, e.g. through questioning and by setting individual and group targets and tasks which will offer appropriate levels of challenge. Some very brief examples of extension possibilities are now given for each of the NLS elements.

Range
(E.g. range: Year 1 Term 1, Non-fiction: signs, labels, captions, lists, instructions.)

- Within each term's recommended range of texts, there are opportunities for diversification. Children can be asked to look at other texts by the same author or texts of similar genres and compare specific literary features. They can compare texts from different cultures. They can classify texts into their genres.

Word level work
(E.g. word level: Year 2 Term 1, Pupils should be taught: To investigate and classify words with the same sounds but different spellings.)

- The objectives for phonological awareness, graphic knowledge and spelling can be based on more complex vocabulary, related to the child's interests to sustain challenge and motivation. Able pupils can deconstruct words, investigate word origins, explore definitions, investigate codes and symbols and look for patterns and word families.

Vocabulary extension
(E.g. vocabulary extension, Year 2 Term 2: Pupils should be taught: to use synonyms and other alternative words/phrases that express same or similar

meanings; to collect, discuss similarities and shades of meaning and use to extend and enhance writing.)

- To fulfil the objectives for vocabulary extension, children can be encouraged to discover more about language use in different contexts and increase their metalinguistic awareness. They can investigate word origins and language change (Kingman Report 1988; Bain 1992; Bunting 1999). They can compare different languages and dialects and explore the nuances of words for themselves. 'More able language users take a greater detailed interest in language. . .' Dean 1998 p. 10)

Handwriting
(E.g. handwriting: Year 4 Term 3, Pupils should be taught: to use a range of presentational skills, e.g. print script for captions, sub-headings and labels; capital letters for posters, title pages, headings; a range of computer-generated fonts and point sizes.)

- The handwriting objectives can be made more challenging by experimenting with different media and by encouraging fluent writers to move towards art work and graphic design.

Sentence level work
(E.g. sentence level: Year 2 Term 3, Pupils should be taught: To turn statements into questions . . . what, where, when, who and to add question marks.)

- Objectives given for grammatical awareness, sentence construction and punctuation can be extended so that able pupils have to hypothesise 'rules' and experiment with syntax to see how meanings are affected. They can analyse sentences and learn to deconstruct language. They can examine syntax and experiment with how punctuation influences meaning.

Text level work
(E.g. fiction and poetry-reading and comprehension Year 4 Term 2. Pupils should be taught: To identify clues which suggest poems are older, e.g. language use, vocabulary, archaic words. E.g. non-fiction – reading and comprehension Year 3 Term 2: To discuss the merits and limitations of instructional texts, including IT and other media texts, and to compare these with others, where appropriate, to give an overall evaluation.)

- Across fiction and non-fiction, the objectives for Reading Comprehension and Writing Composition can be differentiated in terms of process and product and the complexity of the texts used. Able pupils can design their own text-based tasks, constructing and deconstructing texts, to achieve appropriate levels of challenge.

Qualifications Curriculum Authority (QCA) guidance on Speaking and Listening

Teachers have, on the whole, come to value the best elements of the Literacy Strategy and have found ways to adapt the strategy to suit their class and teaching styles, but many regret the initial NLS focus on literacy and neglect of oracy. Alexander (2001), in his comparative study of Primary Education in five countries, identifies an urgent need to: 'transform classroom conversation into an empowering dialogue whose function is cognitive as well as social. Many people still believe that reading and writing are the only 'real' work . . . Such atavism ignores the lessons of modern psychology about the unique contribution of talk to learning . . . We must revisit oracy, and soon . . .'

Fortunately, the QCA (2000b) produced detailed guidelines and a clear framework for the development of Speaking and Listening, with objectives for teaching, allied to age and time, as in the NLS for literacy.

There are four main areas of focus:

- speaking for different audiences;
- listening and responding;
- group interaction and discussion;
- drama and role play.

Teachers are advised to collect evidence of progress, in each area, especially when a contribution is recognised as excellent or significant for a particular child.

The structure of this guidance in Speaking and Listening is particularly helpful for teachers of able pupils in that the *General teaching objective* leads to a *Focus for Teaching*, which in turn leads to advice on *Extending and Reinforcing* the learning.

(Eg. Year 5 Term 2, p. 26)

Listening and responding:
to persuasive language

- identify factual information
- analyse use of language
- identify other methods used to persuade.

Focus for teaching:
listening to broadcast adverts

- identify factual content and features of language used to promote a product, e.g. repetition, emphasis, appeal to listener.

Extending and reinforcing:
- identify occasions in school when language is used to persuade and consider the techniques used (see Figure 2.3).

A group of Year 3 able language users spent some time visiting different classrooms, recording and analysing assemblies, noting persuasive language in the playground and then categorised their examples into different techniques. An evaluation of each persuasive technique, with role plays used to demonstrate each one, was presented in a drama lesson and the teacher recorded significant features.

Figure 2.3 Persuasive language survey (Year 3)

Curriculum 2000

Curriculum 2000 powerfully asserts the potential of the broad curriculum for all pupils. The broad curriculum, as exemplified in the QCA Foundation subjects' schemes of work, is more readily accessed by the able learner and can significantly enhance language capacity. Curriculum 2000 also stresses the importance of English, especially in the promotion of pupils' spiritual, moral, social and cultural development (DfEE 2000, p. 8). Though the examples given are intended for all pupils, they offer useful pointers for enrichment and extension English activities for the able language user.

English provides opportunities to promote:

- spiritual development, through helping pupils represent, explore and reflect on their own and others' inner life in drama and the discussion of texts and ideas;
- moral development, through exploring questions of right and wrong, values and conflict between values in their reading of fiction and non-fiction, in their discussions and in drama;
- social development, through helping pupils collaborate with others to create or present devised or scripted drama and to take account of the needs of the audience and the effects they wish to achieve when adapting their speech and writing, and through reading, reviewing and discussing texts that present issues and relationships between groups and the individual and society in different historical periods and cultures;
- cultural development, through helping pupils explore and reflect on the way that cultures are presented in their stories or poems, through introducing pupils to the English literary heritage, and through learning about language variation in English and how language relates to national, regional and cultural identities.

Gross (1993) suggests that able children are likely to have a keen sense of justice and morality. Through literature, the able reader has often entered into the inner lives of characters and the opportunity to explore spiritual and moral dilemmas and dimensions is something that they respond to well. The following case study (Figure 2.4) involved a group of able children in Year 4, examining moral, social and spiritual dimensions.

A group of children read the story of Joan of Arc which led to role play and the holding of a church council or court. Children were assigned roles as supporters or opponents of Joan, but there were French and English representatives to pose opposing viewpoints. They realised that national loyalties were not the main issue in the debate. What they were discussing was whether Joan was a genuine believer or whether she was making up the voices of God she described.

Interestingly, the group decided that she had been spiritually inspired in some way and decided through a vote, that she was a Saint.

Figure 2.4 Role play and debate (Year 5)

This example revolved around speaking and listening skills. The promotion of key skills through English is a central feature of Curriculum 2000 and an area which affords opportunities to enhance the language curriculum.

These skills include:

- general communication skills;
- ICT skills;
- working with others, e.g. collaborative group work;
- improving own learning and performance;
- problem solving, through group work and drama.

Curriculum 2000 and 'Big ideas'

Curriculum 2000 highlights within English other important aspects of the curriculum, e.g.

- promoting citizenship and thinking skills;
- learning about social, political, historical and cultural contexts which shape and influence the texts pupils read and view;
- developing pupils' ability to put their point of view, question, argue and discuss . . .;
- evaluating critically what they hear, read and view;
- becoming competent users of spoken and written standard English to enable them to participate fully in the wider world beyond school, in public life and in decision making . . . (DfEE 2000, p. 9)

Able children often display a more mature understanding of citizenship issues and social, cultural, moral and political dilemmas and contexts. Citizenship, thinking and debating skills are key features of the Philosophy for Children approach (Lipman 1987). The approach suits most able language users because it involves open-ended discussions which challenge thought. It can be adopted within the literacy hour's shared and guided reading framework.

In Philosophy for Children lessons, the shared text, often a picture book because it can be read as a whole in one lesson, generates questions from the children. These questions are then discussed within a Socratic model of dialogue, (Figure 2.5) where the teacher encourages the pupils to think for themselves and express their views while showing respect for the opinions of others.

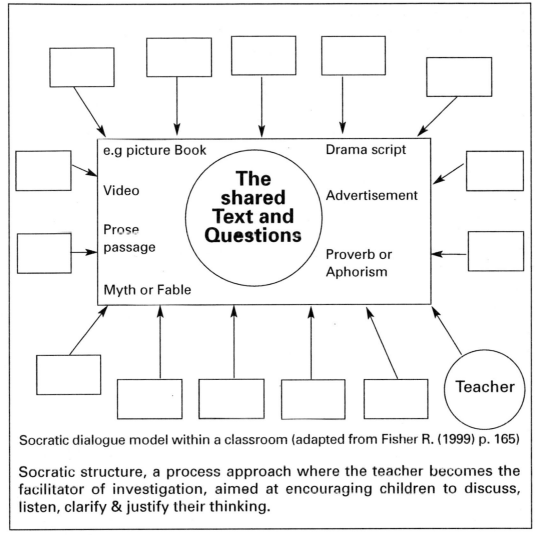

Socratic dialogue model within a classroom (adapted from Fisher R. (1999) p. 165)

Socratic structure, a process approach where the teacher becomes the facilitator of investigation, aimed at encouraging children to discuss, listen, clarify & justify their thinking.

Figure 2.5 Socratic dialogue model within a classroom (Adapted from Fisher 1990 p. 165)

It was in this context that the following questions (Murris 1992) were triggered off by reading *Where the Wild Things Are* by Maurice Sendak:

- What is the difference between dreaming and daydreaming?
- When you are dreaming are you thinking?
- When you are imagining are you thinking?
- Is it possible to be brave and afraid at the same time?
- Are there different ways you can become a king or a queen?
- Do you have to be alone to be lonely?

- Is there an end to every story?
- Do all things that have an end have a beginning?
- Do you think time has a beginning and an end?

Such questions lead children into higher order thinking and discussion of 'big ideas' (time, thought, language, imagination, love, loyalty, bravery, leadership and imponderables, such as an after-life). This adage, found on a classroom wall suggests that we should be encouraging able pupils to discuss 'big ideas' more frequently:

Great people talk about ideas
Average people talk about things
Small people talk about other people

Monitoring the progress of able pupils in English

Anticipation

Schools need to anticipate that in any group of 20–30 children, there may be at least one very able language user. The presence of such children coming into school implies that each school should:

- have a written policy on able pupils;
- have identified resources and strategies to enhance the language curriculum. Ensuring there are texts of an appropriate level of challenge is vital. As Gross (1993) stresses, 'It is ridiculous to suggest that (able) children would gain any benefit or enjoyment from reading, in school, texts which are appropriate in level and content for their age-peers' (p. 187);
- provide INSET on monitoring and promoting the progress of able pupils.

Moderation of children's work – a shared understanding of excellence

Moderating English work across age ranges and ability levels is an important form of staff and school development in that it helps to define attainment, underpins target setting, provides insight into exceptional ability and raises teacher expectations.

Assessment

Able language users' assessments may appear very positive because the children regularly complete assessments to a good standard, for example, they may have 20 out of 20 for every spelling test and be at the top of the scale in verbal reasoning tests and reading assessments.

However, Sainsbury (1996) quotes a teacher who says 'I have some bright children in English who always seem to fulfil my learning intentions. Is this really a significant achievement?'. Sainsbury responds thus: 'Brighter children should be showing as much significant achievement as less able children'. By significant achievement, Sainsbury refers to the communication of meaning across the curriculum in five areas, in which a child's development can be assessed. These areas are:

- physical skills;
- social skills;
- attitude development;
- concepts;
- process skills (p. 31–2).

Sainsbury warns that when an able child frequently, quickly and comfortably completes assessment tasks, it probably means that he/she is not being fully challenged.

Assessment and planning in the Foundation Stage (2–5 years)

At the Foundation Stage, the able language user may already be evident, thanks to their vocabulary and language use and their attitudes towards and skills in literacy. SCAA's Desirable Outcomes publication (1996 p. 10) describes what is expected of a child starting school at five or rising five.

To enhance provision at this stage, there is guidance in the QCA (2000a) for the foundation stage, and much of it focuses on play, e.g. 'The role of the practitioner is crucial in:

- planning and resourcing a challenging environment;
- supporting children's learning through planned play activity;
- extending and supporting children's spontaneous play;
- extending and developing children's language and communication in their play' (p. 25).

Extension is likely to involve the teacher's intervention in the play scenarios to increase the challenge for the more able children. There need to be literacy opportunities and dilemmas which necessitate decision making and discussion. The teacher may slip in and out of role, to create a need to use more sophisticated vocabulary, demand more complex responses and ask the able language user to explain events, justify opinions and hypothesise about outcomes.

Teachers in the foundation stage and early years settings are encouraged to arrange for able pupils to work with others of similar ability occasionally. They are also encouraged to devise collaborative tasks, role play and problem solving and 'help children to talk and plan together about how they will begin, what parts each will play and what materials they will need' (p. 47).

Baseline Assessment

While Baseline Assessment is invariably associated with the process of assessment of children at entry to primary education, it has become an essential part of the evaluation of pupil attainment across the educational spectrum. Schools at all stages have accepted that the availability of detailed data on pupils' attainment and progress provided by assessment at transfer points (e.g. at the end of key stages) provides a critical baseline and source of vital information for evaluation, for planning, for the raising of standards and for the measuring of value added by the school.

Formal assessments – the SATs

The SATs will usually provide confirmation that an able language user, already known to the school, is indeed performing at above average levels. Such information provides the next teacher(s) with important evidence about the child's level of attainment and future learning needs.

However, Eyre (1997) warns that standardised assessments, for example in reading, do not 'allow for the child who is already an accomplished reader and whose reading needs fall far outside what might normally be expected in the reception classroom' (p. 88).

More detailed records of a child's achievements, supported by samples of work, are needed to provide a complete language profile.

Progression in Key Stages 1 and 2 – Records of achievement

A record of achievement which keeps evidence of a child's individual progress is suited to the able child whose abilities lie beyond age-related parameters. Sainsbury (1996) advocates recording significant achievements, with teachers' and/or children's comments reflecting the answers to these two main questions as to 'Why was this significant?' and 'Why did it happen?'.

Self-assessment

Accurate self-assessment depends upon children developing good metacognitive awareness. This can be defined as learners knowing how they know things and the processes by which they think (Fisher 1990). Metacognition uses intrapersonal intelligence (Gardner 1983). It is consistently practised within the literacy hour in the plenary session where children reflect on their learning. Eyre (1997) suggests that 'Of all children they (the able) are the ones who can make the most use of metacognitive information and therefore are likely to benefit from exposure to it' (p. 66).

Target setting

With able children, the process of target setting can and should involve the children themselves, in, for example, the design of an Individual Educational Programme or IEP, in order to meet their learning needs. It is important that the pupil and parents are involved in this, 'helping identify the child's needs and agreeing on ways of meeting them' (Leyden 1998).

Target setting should result in able language users being challenged at their own levels. One strategy is for teachers to introduce more sophisticated 'technical' language into their targets to widen their vocabulary and increase their metalanguage.

Curriculum 2000 (DfEE 2000, p. 44) says that targets for all pupils should:

- build on pupils' knowledge, experiences, interests and strengths to improve areas of weakness and demonstrate progression over time,
- be attainable and yet challenging and help pupils to develop their own self-esteem and confidence and ability to learn.

Teachers of able language users may set individual targets to build upon areas of strength and to develop them to a higher level. The NLS (2000b) has produced some detailed guidance on setting targets for writing and provided examples of targets for each age group: e.g. 'Mentally rehearse writing and re-read as a matter of habit'. Or ' My stories and recounts show the order in which things happened'. Able writers could engage with the targets suggested for older pupils where appropriate.

Above average progress

Able language users may reach these competencies at text, sentence and word level long before their average peers and before the stages and ages prescribed in the NLS Handbook. They may display some or all of the behaviours described and achieve levels in language two to five years ahead of the rest of their class.

Evaluation of work and feedback

Research into assessment by Black (1997) found that the following approaches worked most effectively to raise standards:

- regular formative and non-competitive assessments;
- enhanced feedback, from teacher to pupil;
- active involvement by students, including self-assessment
- careful attention to their motivation and self-esteem.

Teacher comments on written work need to focus on the content, syntax and ideas (the compositional level) and not only on the surface features of spelling, punctuation and presentation (the secretarial level). They can also 'consistently convey high expectations by encouraging pupils to venture further, through a judicious mixture of praise and challenge' (Laar 1997 p. 158).

The following list of criteria for the evaluation of a child's work is adapted from Clark and Callow (1998 pp. 29–30) who suggest several ways to evaluate learning outcomes for the able child:

- **vocabulary and use of words:** e.g. wide choice of words, complex sentence structures and more advanced textual organisation than would be normally expected of a pupil of similar age;
- **analysis, evaluation, judgement:** e.g. evidence offered to support discussion, conflicting viewpoints contrasted, accuracy of information . . .;
- **conceptual understanding:** e.g. understanding of key issues;
- **logic and rigour in reasoning:** e.g. accurate interpretation of sources and opinions justified by reference to texts, other texts;

- **synthesis of complex ideas:** e.g. cogent argument, discussion of alternate points of view;
- **reading level required by sources:** e.g. appropriate for pupil's comprehension abilities;
- **commitment to task:** e.g. motivation, perseverance, care, focus, reflection, ideas for improvement;
- **confidence:** e.g. belief in own abilities, confident approach.

The need to maintain confidence and self-esteem is addressed by Freeman (1998) who highlighted the importance of the teacher's oral feedback in ensuring confidence and commitment to task and motivation.

Some example sof ways teachers can respond to levels of student performance now follow.

Successful performance:

- emphasise the student's abilities or talents – *'The topic/genre suits you'*;
- give consistency information – *'You have done that right again'*;
- give consensus information and thus stress success – *'Most people have difficulties with this . . . but you did it'*.

Unsuccessful performance:

- attribute it to insufficient effort – *'If you read that again, it would soon become clear to you'*.
- take the edge off failure by providing consensus information – *'Most students have difficulties with that'*;
- give distinctiveness information – *'The other topic/genre suits you better doesn't it?'*.

These examples of teacher response suggest the need for positive attitudes towards able pupils in school in order to protect their self-esteem.

The able language user's self-esteem

Mosley (1993) describes self-esteem as 'the inner picture we all have of ourselves. It is the value we give to our strengths and weaknesses'. Most children build their inner picture from the image reflected back to them by their parents, siblings, friends and teachers.

Many able language users have lower self-esteem than might be anicipated because their giftedness has made them different from their peers. They may have demanding and negative parents who have put them under pressure because of unreasonable hopes and expectations. Some able children may sense a lack of continuity between the values at home and school. It is not unknown to perceive teachers who seem to see able language users as precocious, demanding and almost a 'burden' in that they demand different provision.

It is vital that the child perceives that the important adults in his/her life are working together to provide encouragement, to build the child's self-esteem and to offer, in partnership, the richest, most enjoyable and fulfilling language curriculum they can.

Enhancing the English curriculum for gifted pupils

A language enhancing environment and ethos

A school where language is valued will have a language-rich environment and will devote time and resources to ensure the quantity, quality, range and challenge of suitable texts in the school. The attitudes of the staff towards language, from pupil-adult interaction to the celebration of success and excellence will be influential. Some schools try to raise children's awareness of languages in general by featuring a language of the week and by encouraging all pupils to learn a few phrases or words (Gibbon 1994).

Organisational strategies

There are various organisational strategies, linked to teaching styles, that are likely to benefit able language users:

- **Acceleration:** the able child is moved into a different group for part of the curriculum, e.g. the literacy hour.
- **Setting:** some schools, especially larger primary schools or those with vertically-grouped classes, have introduced setting based on assessments such as SATs.
- **Grouping by ability:** so that in guided and independent reading and writing sessions, the most able children perform different tasks or use more difficult texts.
- **Individually negotiated tasks:** 'If we are keen to encourage children to think, then establishing a climate where it is possible to negotiate an adaptation to the set class task is one way to facilitate this' (Eyre 1997). Similarly, Blake (1995) found that involving the pupils in exploring ways to increase the challenge within a task or project was very successful in providing for the able pupils.
- **Collaborative groupwork:** a similar approach is common in structured collaborative groupwork where children discuss how they will do a task and review and analyse the processes needed for effective groupwork. Interestingly, one of the likely benefits for able pupils is that they learn to value other children's contributions more highly because, in certain tasks, it is clear that academic abilities may not be the most useful. Guided reading and writing sessions may often promote collaborative response and action.
- **Core plus options:** able children complete the same core asks as the others but are then offered a choice of activity or a more challenging extension activity.
- **Plan/Do/Review:** the High/Scope approach to learning development, initially developed in the USA, encourages preschool children to assume greater responsibility for their learning. Children have to plan, do and review their

learning each day. The strategy works well for able pupils in English in that it encourages independent literacy behaviours and good communication skills.

- **Enriching the language curriculum:** enrichment of the curriculum implies a broadening of the content, a greater variety of approaches, processes and experiences, whereby able pupils are given *more* stimulus, e.g. a wider range of texts, genres and audience.
- **Extending the language curriculum:** Extension refers to a deepening of the curriculum. It enables pupils to explore issues, examine connections, analyse similarities and differences, discover subtleties and nuances, and generally see more, e.g. in a picture book, by looking longer and by asking different and deeper questions, to explore inference and implication.

The framework of questions devised by the International Schools' Curriculum Project, now adopted by the International Baccalaureate Primary Years Programme (IBPYP 1999) provides us with an enquiry-based model for learning about any subject. The curriculum framework was designed, in the late 1990s, by teachers working in international schools and is intended to be culturally open-ended so that it can be applied in any context. The framework revolves around the following questions:

- What's it like?
- How does it work?
- Why is it like it is?
- How is it changing?
- How is it connected to other things?
- What are the points of view?
- How do we know?

These questions can be applied to any area of learning and can encourage the learner to engage more profoundly with the subject.

Teaching styles

Good teachers of English vary, but over 20 years ago Galton and Simon and Croll's ORACLE Project (1980) identified one particular teaching style which has been recognised as particularly effective for able pupils. Teachers described as 'class enquirers' challenged and questioned their children, often on a whole class basis, and moved around giving feedback and developing and discussing work in progress. This style of teaching is very similar to that described in the NLS handbook which describes the most successful teaching as:

- discursive – characterised by high quality oral work and questioning;
- interactive – with pupils' contributions encouraged, expected and extended;
- well-paced – there is a sense of urgency, driven by the need to make progress and succeed;
- confident – teachers have a clear understanding of the objectives and good subject knowledge;
- ambitious – there is optimism about and high expectations of success (p. 8).

Particularly relevant is the emphasis on oral work. Able pupils are, in many ways, like all other children. They like to have their good ideas acknowledged and their best efforts praised. They like to enjoy themselves too, and a teaching style, characterised by pace and humour as well as challenge, will encourage them to do their best.

Enquiry-based learning

Teachers are accustomed to questioning pupils and soliciting their answers but may not devote as much effort to encourage pupils' questions. Searching, open questions which help develop higher order thinking skills (Bloom 1956) challenge children to think more deeply. Pupils' questions can provide teachers with valuable information as a basis for their planning. Harnessing pupils' natural desire to find out more about their world can be a self-differentiating approach.

Able pupils are likely to have knowledge, interests and enthusiasms and areas where they may have developed significant expertise and much of this may be unknown to their teachers. It is important to assess what pupils already know about a research topic before starting (see Figure 2.6).

When the teacher of a vertically grouped class introduced a new topic, she would give out up to six slips of paper or card and ask the children to write down three things they already knew about the topic and three questions about it, to which they would like to know the answers before the topic was over. These pieces of paper provided the teacher with a substantial appreciation of the levels of understanding across the class. It enabled her to give the children ownership of their learning and the slips of paper formed a useful temporary display, which served to inform parents about the topic. Sometimes, the teacher used the questions as a basis for reference skills development, with the questions serving as headings in a large class book (made from a scrapbook) about the topic.

The approach allowed the able pupils to work at their own level. Their questions and their ensuing research were invariably more sophisticated.

Figure 2.6 Assessing prior knowledge

A variation of this is the 'inversion' of the conventional teacher sets questions and children give answers model, so that the teacher gives the answer and the children set the questions.

This example is based on NLS Year 6 Term 3:

Pupils should be taught to divide whole texts into paragraphs, paying attention to the sequence of paragraphs and to the links between one paragraph and the next, e.g. through the choice of appropriate connectives' (p. 55).

- *Teacher's answer:* 'Next, meanwhile, eventually, ultimately, before . . .'
- *Children's question:* 'Which words (connectives) link ideas and suggest time?'
- *Writing composition task:* Write a recount about an incident in the playground. Use paragraphs and try to use all or some of the connectives.

Finally teachers can encourage divergent thought by asking and displaying hypothetical questions.

Examples of such hypothetical questions might include:

- Suppose we . . .?
- What if . . .?
- Is it always true that . . .?
- How much evidence is there . . .?
- Can you imagine . . .?
- Are there any alternatives . . .?
- What are the exceptions . . .?
- How could it be different . . .?
- Would you rather . . . or . . .?
- How could it be improved . . .?

Problem solving in English

Vygotsky (1978) introduced the concept of the ZPD, or Zone of Proximal Development alongside an emphasis on collaborative and cooperative learning, where learning is seen as a social activity, focused around cooperative problem solving. He proposed that the only 'good learning' is 'that which is in advance of development'. Learning occurs in the space between the problem solving which a child can carry out independently and that for which they need the support and guidance of others, e.g adults or peers. 'What a child can do in co-operation today, he can do alone tomorrow' (Vygotsky 1978). This would point to the potential benefit of enabling able pupils to work collaboratively with their intellectual peers and those who are developmentally slightly ahead of them.

De Bono (1972) sees problem solving as representative of other thinking processes and a 'convenient way to demonstrate these processes' (p. 11). For de Bono, problem solving is synonymous with 'dealing with a situation', 'overcoming an obstacle', 'bringing about a desired effect' and 'making something happen'. It could be said that these attributes are certainly present in educational drama and in many literacy tasks.

Clark and Callow (1998 p. 33) stress the usefulness of problem solving to provide challenge for able children. They offer a simple model for problem solving.

- Stage 1: Problem recognition
- Stage 2: Goal definition
- Stage 3: Information collection
- Stage 4: Hypothesis production

- Stage 5: Selection of the most effective line of enquiry
- Stage 6: Solution
- Stage 7: Examination of the solution for its implications

This model, like De Bono's, is conspicuously suited to English, especially in role play and drama, language study and non-fiction activities. Able pupils sometimes feel more comfortable about their abilities when working with children who are not their direct peers. Problem-solving projects with younger pupils might include: making reading games based upon picture books; writing and presenting historical plays; arranging scientific investigations for them; helping them make maps; designing and making toys or conducting surveys.

Higher order thinking skills

Bloom's (1956) framework, put simplistically, moves the thinker from *knowing that* through *knowing how* to *knowing why* (see Appendix One). When planning for a group of more able children or an individual able language user, it is helpful to consider how to ensure increasing levels of complexity. Here are examples of Bloom's (1956) taxonomy applied to language study in each key stage (see Table 2.1).

Table 2.1 Bloom's taxonomy of Thinking Skills applied to English

KS1 examples

Level of thinking	Example
Knowledge	Read the Big Book and write down all the words which mean *say* or *said*.
Comprehension	Put the words in order of loudness, starting with *whispered*.
Application	Make a list of words which can be used to show someone speaking and use them in sentences of your own.
Analysis	Find some of these words in your friend's storybook. See if you agree with the writer about his/her choice of word.
Synthesis	Act out some sentences for the class/another group/each other and see whether they can guess the word used from the way you speak, e.g. *mumbled*.
Evaluation	Here are two short stories. They are the same but one has a variety of words for speaking. The other only uses *said*. Write about the difference between the stories.

KS2 examples

Level of thinking	Example
Knowledge	What's the difference between a metaphor and a simile?
Comprehension	Read this poem and underline the metaphors. Explain the effect of each one.
Application	Make up metaphors to describe an animal of your own choice.
Analysis	Read some more poems in an anthology. Find some (5? 10?) more metaphors and explain why the poet used each one.
Synthesis	Write a definition of a metaphor. Try to write a short story using metaphors to replace every noun.
Evaluation	In which ways are metaphors useful? List all the reasons why the world would be a poorer place without metaphors.

Able pupils, if encouraged to become aware of these levels of thinking as they engage with a topic in English, can find them useful in reference or library skills, where they skim and scan texts for information and analyse the data gathered before synthesising it into some form of presentation (e.g. poster, report, summary, flier, newsflash).

Study skills and concept mapping

Learning how to learn and how to study effectively is as important for able pupils as their peers. Notetaking, revising for recall, summarising key points, brainstorming and concept mapping are strategies which need to be practised and refined. Concept mapping or mind mapping (Buzan 1988) has three main purposes:

- to explore what the learner knows, identifying key concepts and the connections between them;
- to help planning, by organising ideas and showing links between them;
- to aid evaluation, by reflecting on what we know (Fisher 1995).

Concept mapping can provide indicators of the extent of children's learning and understanding. Following is an example, Figure 2.7, from a six year old, mapping out his conceptual understanding of reading.

Reading

A gifted reader is one who may:

- read more quickly;
- demonstrate strong predictive and deductive skills;
- have excellent, even photographic, recall of the text;

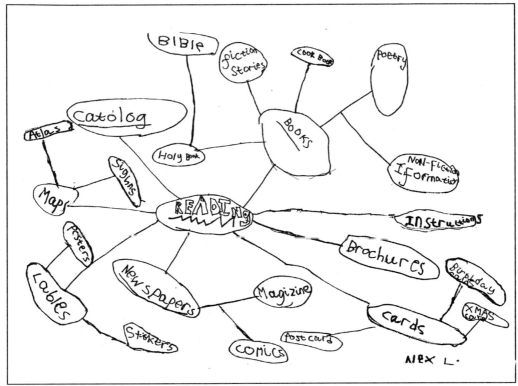

Figure 2.7 Concept map of reading (Year 2)

- understand the literal and inferential meanings of a text;
- be able to empathise with the characters in a story;
- be able to synthesise information from a variety of sources;
- be able to justify reading preferences.

Simply increasing the number or variety of books read is unlikely, alone, to help able readers develop in terms of their critical response, so that they are capable of reading at different levels, able to discriminate, evaluate and to formulate judgements. They need opportunities for regular sharing, discussion and trained analysis of literature with able peers and informed adults.

The NLS has provided opportunities for critical exploration of worthwhile and challenging texts. Many teachers are using interactive books on CD-Rom and a range of language-based software to promote critical reading in and beyond the literacy hour. Teachers may be able to arrange for older pupils to become 'book buddies' for younger able readers.

Shared reading

The searchlights model (Figure 2.8) shows how important it is that the whole class shared text is not too easy for the able child. It must provide challenge, so that the knowledge of the able child is extended or expanded in one of the areas shown, e.g. grammatical knowledge.

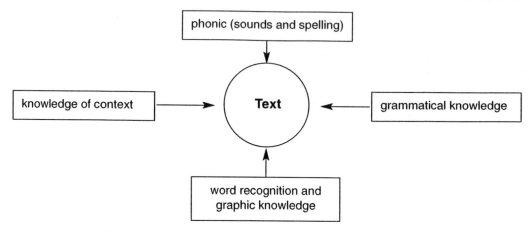

Figure 2.8 Searchlights model (NLS *Handbook* 1999)

Guidance to teachers on selecting texts for shared reading is that they should choose a text that it is beyond the ability of the majority of the class to read by themselves, thus providing them with a new challenge. However, there is a danger that even a text which stretches the majority of the class will still not be sufficiently challenging for the most able pupils.

Guided reading

The emphasis in guided reading is on three kinds of comprehension questions which can challenge the able reader:

- literal questions;
- inferential questions;
- evaluative questions.

(First Steps 1999 p. 66)

Teachers need to encourage able readers to respond divergently to texts and to read 'creatively' (Labuda 1977) so that they interpret and reconstruct the text for themselves. Able pupils can be encouraged in fiction, poetry and playscripts to focus on inference, characterisation and seminal points in narrative; to develop critical analysis skills and to make suggestions and frameworks for possible sequels, e.g. the next *Harry Potter*. In non-fiction, they can be encouraged to distinguish fact from opinion, compare texts and to synthesise information.

The use of DARTS (Directed Activities Related to Texts (Lunzer *et al.* 1984)) can challenge pupils to read texts more critically. There are two main categories of DART:

- reconstructive, where the original text has been modified by the teacher and the pupils have to reconstruct it, e.g. cloze with words deleted, sequencing jumbled paragraphs, substituting nonsense words, etc.

- transformative, where the text is complete but the pupils have to transform it or interrogate it in some way, e.g. highlighting key points, question-setting, interpreting the text as a diagram, etc.

First Steps (1999) reading materials offer a wide range of DART activities across both key stages and in a range of genres, including non-fiction.

Reading and writing non-fiction

There are three main categories of non-fiction:

- Narrative – information stories, biographies, procedural writing, recounts and reports.
- Reference – dictionaries, thesauruses, encyclopaedias, atlases.
- Information books – non-story picture books, catalogues, information books (Mallett 1992 p. 21).

In order to make progress in their reading and writing of these genres, teacher mediation between able pupils and the texts is essential. Eyre points out (1997 p. 54) that a teacher saying, 'Go and find out all you can about . . .' is unlikely to lead to extensive use of research skills and instead may lead to disruption in the library. Differentiation in research skills can be planned according to the starting point rather than by outcome, and one way of doing this is by the use of grids. These help children to organise their thinking by teaching them to set purposes for their research and help them to assimilate the information.

The KWL grid, developed by Ogle and Blachowicz (1989), helps children set out their purposes for reading, and then make notes of what they learn. The grid is composed of three columns in which children answer the questions, What do I KNOW? What do I WANT to find out? and What did I LEARN? Relating what children have learnt to what they set out to learn helps them to structure their reading-based enquiry and avoid the habit of merely copying chunks of text from reference books.

Writing frames

Wray and Lewis's (1999) writing frames have a similar purpose. These are particularly suitable for use with able pupils as teachers can adapt them by putting in additional specific questions, as in the adapted model below:

- Although I already knew that . . .
- I have learnt some new facts. I learnt that . . .
- I also learnt that . . .
- Another fact I learnt . . .
- However, the most interesting thing I learnt was . . .
- I would now like to find out more about . . .

The frames help children to organise the information they glean from several sources and support them in producing a coherent and logically ordered piece of non-fiction writing. The results may sometimes be stilted, but able pupils can be encouraged to go further and give more thought to the quality of their writing as well.

They could also be asked to 'restructure' the text into a different form. This involves presenting what they have learnt in a different way and again helps children to assimilate the facts and avoid copying from reference books. Possible ways of restructuring are:

- a job advert (e.g. 'Governess Wanted' by rich Victorian mill owner);
- a letter home;
- a newspaper report;
- a diary entry;
- a chart.

Gifted pupils are likely to respond successfully to the demands of non-narrative writing. They will be able to identify key points, summarise evidence and convey it clearly, maintain an argument or line of reasoning, and report accurately to inform and instruct.

Teachers can help them to enhance such skills by:

- ensuring the types and structures of non-narrative forms are familiar to pupils through consistent analysis of complete texts rather than through decontextualised exercises;
- making sure that non-narrative writing assignments have a clear and worthwhile purpose;
- giving assignments which are of interest and concern to the writer, e.g. being persuasive about causes that matter to them;
- ensuring that alternative viewpoints are considered;
- finding in the broad curriculum the basis for many of the non-narrative forms (see QCA).

Reading and responding to literature

Where literature is concerned, able readers are fortunate that they can access the wealth and riches of fiction about characters from different cultures and time periods.

Warlow's (1974) overview of literary genres may serve as a useful guide for extending able readers. Each genre of fiction requires different reading strategies and could extend able children in learning how to appreciate or deconstruct and interrogate texts (Derewianka 1990, Hourihan 1997) in greater depth.

Gifted readers tend to read books which are aimed at average children who may be 3–7 years older. It must be stressed however that while it may be appropriate to enable children to move on towards older, even adult fiction, it is helpful to remember that the text itself is less important in learning than the way it is used. Particular picture books like those of Anthony Browne, John Burningham, Philip Dupasquier, *The Ultimate Alphabet*, Quentin Blake's *Clown*, McKewan's *Rose*

Blanche, Oakley's *Henry's Quest* or Noon's *A Street Through Time* can provide rich, intriguing and complex experiences for able readers at both Key Stages. As Baddeley and Eddershaw (1994), who used picture books to challenge thought and discussion with 4–12 year olds, reflect, 'Indeed the ten and eleven year olds we worked with sometimes approached a level of attainment comparable to what is required for the study of adult literature' (p.75).

Book talk

In order to extend and develop children's critical facility in discussing their own and others' texts, it may be useful to consider not only the philosophy for children approach to questioning, but also Chambers' (1993) 'Tell Me' framework of questions (pp. 83–92). Some examples of such questions include: 'What will you tell your friends about it?', 'Was there anything that puzzled you?', 'Tell me about the parts you liked the most', 'If the author asked you what could be improved in the story, what would you say?.'

Again, First Steps resource materials on reading (1999) contain many worthwhile strategies which could be used to extend able children's response to stories, poems and plays.

Writing

If there is an aspect of English where able children's ability should be most evident, it is writing. With their extensive vocabulary, familiarity with the writing of others and their sensitivity to language nuances, their writing is likely to be more mature than their peers. However, even able pupils may reflect a recognisable difference in performance between their reading and writing abilities, a difference which has been evident in national SAT tests at all key stages.

Successful performance is far more difficult to achieve in writing because reading is a more 'receptive' process, despite the fact that readers bring their knowledge about language, books and life to any textual encounter. Writing is a 'productive' process, wherein writers encode meanings. It involves challenging motor skills; engagement with and memory of the arbitrary nature of written conventions and the vagaries of English spelling; awareness of the purposes for writing; experience of writing in different genres; appreciation of the relationships between reading and writing and speech and writing and the need to consider an audience.

Shared and guided writing

Modelling the writing process (e.g. teacher demonstration and teacher scribing) is the main purpose of shared writing and is the principal means of teaching writing in the literacy hour. In guided writing, the emphasis is on planning and drafting, revising and editing or polishing writing, in terms of *text cohesion, sentence construction, punctuation, word choice and modification*. It should enable teachers *'to work intensively with able writers on composing or editing a draft'* (NLS 2000b p. 18). The key word here is intensively. Ten minutes of challenging interaction about their current piece of writing can effectively challenge an able writer and help them to reflect more deeply upon the quality of the genre, the language, the syntax and all the other elements of writing.

Teachers can cultivate able children's ability to write by:

- Providing a wide range of quality written texts. The children should hear texts being read aloud and see them being constructed and analysed in shared writing.
- Encouraging them to maintain a personal writer's journal.
- Using think books (Bicknell, in Fisher 1990) where pupils engage in 'explorative writing – asking questions and attempting answers' can be helpful with able language users, because they are writing independently and are able to write at their level, open-endedly and without the pressure of public presentation.
- Working with them to enhance their own writing. Independent writing sessions in the literacy hour need to serve as 'writing conferences' Graves (1983), where teachers can provide individual feedback and encourage reflection on children's writing.
- Ensuring systematic use of shared and guided writing sessions to enhance pupils' use of main sentence forms.
- Providing children with a thorough grounding in grammar. Mastery of grammar is cognitively demanding and is more likely to be accessible to the able child. (NLS *Grammar for Writing* 2000).
- Helping them to develop study skills. Pupils should also be taught 'to use writing to help their thinking, investigating, organising and learning' (DfEE 2000 p. 29). Writing can be used to support learning. We can learn about the way we think by writing down our thoughts. This is known as cognitive writing and involves 'such processes as abstracting general principles, making inferences' (Fisher 1999 p. 59)
- Structuring the week so that children can write for sustained periods. Able children need an opportunity not only to write longer pieces, but also to spend extended time drafting their work, in discussion with their intellectual peers or adults, with an emphasis on improvement.
- Systematically mediating children's encounters with texts and helping them to become aware of the differences between narrative and non-narrative forms.

Writing stories

The able language user is likely to attempt long and complex narratives. Unless teachers consciously develop narrative skills, however, the literary qualities of their writing may not progress. From storyboards to plot profiles, there are many resources and strategies to develop narrative.

In First Steps (Writing Developmental Continuum 1999b) there is a helpful overview of narrative indicators which teachers can use to identify the child's narrative needs and see which teaching strategies may move the child on.

The NLS (2000b) has recently given teachers excellent guidance on the teaching of writing, with many opportunities for extension which would challenge able writers, as in this narrative-based example:

Unit 38, where the objective for Year 5, Term1 T14 is:

> To map out texts showing development of structure, e.g. its high and low points, the links between sections, paragraphs, chapters.

A teacher, working on narrative skills could use the sample task given where children have to 'box' the story segments and plan 'paragraph prompts'.

The guidance suggests that children can explore the concepts of:

- parallel narrative structure;
- a story within a story;
- time-slip narrative;
- complex narrative with non-linear chronology.

One way able children could explore the different forms could be visual. Examples could be taken from TV as well as books. Able children could experiment with writing their own narratives with these structures. Teachers can enhance their able pupils' narrative skills by helping them understand that successful narrative writing is grounded in personal and familiar experience and by acquainting pupils with the handful of themes that underpin most narrative and the main elements of narrative:

- coherence of plot;
- successful use of crises, conflict and denouement;
- the creation of settings;
- the management of time inside the story;
- the development of characters;
- the power of narratives based on the commonplace and arising from personal experience.

In the following example, the teacher was anxious to help pupils understand that effective narrative came often not from the bizarre, the spectacular or the contrived, but from the ordinary made memorable and from distortion, however slight, of the predictable, (Figure 2.9).

Writing poetry

This is a writing genre that may be particularly suited to the capabilities of gifted children because they usually enjoy the very sound of language and the opportunity to combine words and phrases in original ways. They may, however, need as much initial support and inspiration as other children. Children's ability to write poetry is often dependent on the extent of their acquaintance with the work of established poets and their awareness of the ways in which poets use and manipulate language to create effects and shape meanings.

It is helpful to ask the children to discuss the nature of poetry, e.g.

'It's like writing the words from the inside out . . . to express how you feel.'
'I think it's like a dance of words and ideas – there's got to be some music, see?'

A Year 6 class had worked intensively over a period of half a dozen lessons or so on the construction of narrative, focusing on essential elements: theme, plot structure and development including issues of problems/conflict, crises, resolutions and denouement; settings and characterisation. This work included an exploration of the variations of form called for by different genres – e.g. romantic, historical, comic, adventure, mystery – within narrative.

The teacher felt that the ghost story genre, as exemplified in classic examples of the form, best represented what she was seeking to teach, with the most powerful effects often located or concealed in the most routine of circumstances.

After hearing several examples, the class then worked, in shared writing to make a sequence of routine events, everyday situations and commonplace environments assume an eerie, disturbing or inexplicable significance. They then constructed, over four lessons, the story of a school haunted by the apparition of a nondescript man seen, in his fleeting visitations, gazing fixedly and mournfully at school photographs in an isolated corridor of the school.

Pupils were then required to create, individually, 'extended' ghost or mystery stories based on a range of 'brainstormed' ideas.

Figure 2.9 Writing a good story (Year 6)

It is also valuable to identify the stages required to write a poem. Children may generate a list similar to this list, which can also be used to develop critical responses to and analysis of the poetry of others:

- Be inspired: *What do I want to say?*
- Brainstorm: *Which words can I use?*
- Have a go: *Which ideas and where?*
- Draft it: *How does it look?*
- Read it aloud: *How does it sound?*
- Revise it: *How can I improve it?*
- Proof read: *Can other people read and understand it?*
- Present it: *Who's it for and how shall I present it?*

Just as writing frames can be invaluable for developing non-fiction and storyboards for narrative, in poetry some form of scaffolding or framework can be very helpful and less constrictive than may first appear. Acrostics and haiku are much-used frameworks but there are many others, e.g. tanka, diamond poems, limericks, sonnets, kennings and poems which are triggered off by repetitive phrases or questions.

Using ICT for writing

Tolstoy (1862) once wrote that the business of the teacher is to help pupils access all known and unknown methods that may make learning easier for them. The capacities of the word processor have certainly made redrafting and editing a less daunting process for writers. All children respond well to seeing their ideas 'published' and legible enough for their peers to share. Other opportunities offered by ICT can be found in Chapter 5.

Drama

'At one end of the spectrum there is spontaneous role play where the child is experimenting with language and actions which may never be repeated the same way. At the opposite end we might have the same child performing a practised role in front of an audience of parents' (Clipson-Boyles, in Bentley *et al.* 1999 p. 159). Drama is an important part of a language-enhancing curriculum. It can add another dimension to reading and writing tasks:

1. beforehand, as a form of rehearsal of ideas and feelings;
2. during, as a way of bringing a task to life;
3. afterwards, to synthesise what has been learnt.

It can support able pupils in their understanding of literature, including Shakespeare, where they can engage with rich language textures and 'big ideas', such as kingship, pathos, irony, ambition, jealousy and love. Drama develops talking and thinking through:

- metaphor;
- symbols;
- role;
- emotions.

(Neelands 1992 p. 26)

It offers able children in particular a relatively 'safe' context in which to explore their emotions, an audience for their writing and combines several intelligences, including the interpersonal and intrapersonal (Gardner 1983).

Able pupils may respond particularly well to meeting real-life actors. This is perhaps because they empathise with sometimes having to pretend to be someone else (i.e., able children downplaying their strengths to be accepted by the peer group), the uniqueness actors so often strive for and the extra attention actors receive. Inviting professional actors and theatre-in-education groups to talk about their work can be very rewarding. Many local theatres also offer after school drama workshops or education programmes.

Opportunities beyond the conventional curriculum

Experts in English and enrichment days

All pupils deserve to encounter those who demonstrate excellence in English, e.g. playwrights, public speakers, poets, storytellers, calligraphers, editors, authors and copywriters. Able pupils can be asked to prepare for such a visit in more depth, researching the areas of visitors' expertise and devising questions for them.

Sometimes, it may be possible to arrange visits or field trips to places where English is being used for a specific purpose, e.g. the law courts, a publishing house, an advertising agency or radio station.

Clubs and competitions

Readers' and writers' clubs can encourage more able children to build upon their interest in language. They can create a literary circle, where they invite groups of children to read and discuss books and their own writing. Devising school-wide competitions for poetry, non-fiction, stories or radio plays helps schools to highlight quality in language. A school magazine or yearbook is another important vehicle for the celebration of excellence and originality. It can also offer able children problem solving and collaborative activity.

The home-school partnership

Parents of able language users are likely to react in one of two ways to their child's giftedness. They may be delighted and supportive, because they prize language competence, enjoy books themselves and be keen for their child to excel in some area of the curriculum. Many able children's parents involve themselves in the school and make every effort to understand and enrich the curriculum. Conversely, however, parents may feel threatened because they feel their own language or academic skills are underdeveloped. They may feel a sense of helplessness because they are unsure how best to develop their child's talents and need guidance about suitable books and language opportunities.

Parental support for the school is often dependent on the way parents of able pupils perceive their children are being challenged and encouraged. For the children's sake, it is vital schools work in partnership with parents so that able language users' needs are fulfilled.

Schools can advise parents on the many good resources and educational opportunities (e.g. community and library events) which are available.

Support can include:

- the resources available in the home. In Gross' study (1993) the parents of gifted children owned a great more books (500–1000) than the control families.
- placing limits on certain activities, such as TV, in order to enable children time for imaginative and exploratory play, reading, writing and drawing. Researchers have discovered that gifted children watch two hours less TV per day than their control peers. The parents of the gifted children were more likely to become involved in their children's interpretation and use of TV and media information. The parents of able children tend to interact with their children about the issues unfolding before them on the screen and then discuss the issues raised.

Homework

Parents of able language users generally will not need to spend as long listening to their child decoding text on a regular basis but they can be encouraged to continue their 'reading times' in order to discuss their child's reading at increasingly complex levels. They can be given support materials, e.g. with ideas for inferential comprehension and a variety texts, language games, word searches and linguistic challenges which are just beyond their child's independent capability.

Summary

In this chapter we have considered the influences on and the issues affecting the able language user at home and school. Able children need and deserve more from their teachers than 'They're bright. They're always reading. They'll be okay . . .'. Evidence (Eyre 1997) shows that able pupils may not thrive if left to underachieve.

The resources and strategies now available, combined with a deepening understanding of learning styles (Smith 1998) should mean that able language users can feel valued by their schools and fulfilled and excited by what awaits them in their English lessons and by the linguistic and intellectual adventures they can share with their teachers.

'The wise teacher does not ask you to enter the house of his wisdom. He leads you the threshold of your own mind' (Kahlil Gibran 1995).

References

Alexander, R. (2001) *Culture and Pedagogy: International Comparisons in Primary Education*. Oxford: Blackwell.

Baddeley, P. and Eddershaw, C. (1994) *Not So Simple Picture Books: Developing Responses to Literature With 4-12 year olds*. Stoke-on-Trent: Trentham Books.

Bain, R. (1992) *Looking into Language: Classroom approaches to knowledge about language*. London: Hodder and Stoughton.

Bentley, D. *et al.* (1999) *The Really Practical Guide to Primary English*. Cheltenham: Stanley Thornes.

Black, P. J. (1997) *Testing: friend or foe? Theory and practice of assessment and testing*. London: Falmer.

Bloom, B. S. (1956) *Taxonomy of Educational Objectives. Volume 1*. London: Longman.

Brice-Heath, S. (1983) *Ways with Words: Language, Life and Work in Communities and Classrooms*. Cambridge: CUP.

Bruner, J. (1986) *Actual Minds. Possible Worlds*. Cambridge, Mass: Harvard University Press.

Buzan, T. (1988) *Make the Most of Your Mind*. London: Pan Books.

Chambers, A. (1993) *Tell Me: Children, Reading and Talk*. STROUD: Thimble Press.

Clark, C. and Callow, R. (1998) *Educating Able Children*. London: NACE/Fulton.

De Bono, E. (1972) *Children Solve Problems*. Harmondsworth: Penguin.

Dean, G. (1999) *Challenging the More Able Language User*. London: NACE/Fulton.

Derewianka, B. (1990) *Exploring the Writing of Genres.* NSW, Australia: PETA

DfEE (2000) *Curriculum 2000 English.* London: HMSO.

Evans, L. and Goodhew, G. (1997) *Providing for Able Children; Activities for Staff in Primary and Secondary Schools.* Oxford: Framework Press.

Eyre, D. (1997) *Able Children in Ordinary Schools.* London: David Fulton Publishers.

Fisher, R. (1990) *Teaching Children to Think.* Hemel Hempstead: Simon and Schuster.

Fisher, R. (1995) *Teaching Children to Learn.* Cheltenham: Stanley Thornes.

First Steps (1999a) *Shared and Guided Reading and Writing: 1 and 2.* London: Ginn Heinemann.

First Steps (1999) *Literacy Developmental Continuum.* London: Ginn Heinemann.

Fowler (1990) in Howe M. J. A. (edn) *Encouraging the Development of Exceptional Skills and Talents.* London: British Psychological Society.

Freeman, J. (1998) *Educating the Very Able: Current International Research.* London: OFSTED/HMSO.

Galton, M. Simon, B and Croll, P. (1980) *Inside the Primary Classroom.* London: Routledge and Kegan Paul.

Gardner, H. (1983) *Frames of Mind.* London: Fontana.

Gawith, G. (1987) *Library Alive!: Promoting Reading and Research in the School Library.* London: A & C Black Ltd.

Gawith, G. (1989) *Reading Alive!* London: A & C Black Ltd.

Gibbon, P. (1994) *Learning to Learn in a Second Language.* NSW, Australia: PETA.

Gibran, Kahil (1995) *The Prophet* (Introduction by S. Bushuai). Oxford.

Goswami, U. and Bryant, P. (1990) *Phonological Skills and Learning to Read.* Hove: Laurence Erlbaum Associates.

Graham, J. and Kelly, A. (1997) *Reading Under Control.* David Fulton/ Roehampton Institute.

Graves, D. (1983) *Writing: Teachers and Children at Work.* Oxford: Heinemann.

Gross, M. U. M. (1993) *Exceptionally Gifted Children.* London: Routledge.

Hourihan (1997) *Deconstructing the Hero.* London: Routledge.

International Baccalaureate Organisation (1999) *Primary Years Programme.* Geneva, Switzerland: IBO.

Kingman Report (1988) *Committee of Inquiry into the Teaching of English Language.* London: HMSO.

Laar, B. (1997) *Guide to Surviving School Inspection.* London: TES/Butterworth Heinemann

Labuda, M. (1977) *Creative Reading for Gifted Learners: A Design for Excellence.* Newark, International Reading Association.

Lee-Corbin, H. and Denicolo, P. (1998) *Able Children in Primary Schools.* London: David Fulton Publishers.

Leyden, S. (1998) *Supporting the Child of Exceptional Ability.* London: Nace/ Fulton.

Lipman, M. (1987) *Philosophy for Children.* Philadelphia: Temple University Press.

Lunzer, E., Gardner, K., Davies, F. and Greene, T. (1984) *Learning from the Written Word.* London: Oliver Boyd.

Mallett, M. (1992) *Making Facts Matter – Reading Non-fiction 5–11.* London: Paul Chapman.

Montgomery, D. (1996) *Educating the Able.* London: Cassell.

Mosley, J. (1993) *Turn your school round.* New York: LDA.

Murris, K. (1992) *Teaching Philosophy with Picture Books.* London: Infonet.

National Literacy Strategy Framework (1999) *Handbook.* London: HMSO.

NLS/DfEE (2000) Grammar for Writing Guidance. London: DfEE.

Neelands, J. (1992) *Developing Imagined Experience.* London: Hodder.

Ogle, D. and Blachowicz, C. (1989) *Reading Comprehension.* Guildford: Guildford Press.

QCA (2000a): *English Within Foundation Subjects.* London: HMSO.

QCA (2000b) *Guidance re Speaking and Listening.* London: HMSO.

QCA (2000c) *Guidance re More Able Pupils (English).* London: HMSO.

Sainsbury, M. (1996) *Tracking Significant Achievement.* Buckingham: Open University Press.

SCAA (1996) *Nursery Education: Desirable Outcomes for Children Entering Compulsory Education.* London: SCAA/DfEE.

Shaw, S. and Hawes, R. (1998) *Effective Teaching and Learning in the Primary Classroom – A Practical Guide to Brain Compatible Learning.* Leicester: Optimal Learning Press.

Vygotsky, L.S. (1978) *Mind in Society.* Cambridge Mass.: Harvard University Press.

Smith, A. (1998) *Accelerated Learning in Practice.* Stafford: Network Educational Press.

Wallace, B. (2000) *Teaching the Very Able Child.* London: Ward Lock Educational.

Warlow, A. (1974) in Meek, M. *The Cool Web.* London: Bodley Head.

Wells, G. (1987) *The Meaning Makers.* London: Heinemann.

Resources

Allen, R. and Skitt, C. (1998) *Mensa Book of Puzzles and Challenges.* London: Dorling Kindersley.

Augarde, T. (1986) *The Oxford Guide to Word Games.* Oxford: OUP.

Berger-Kaye, C. (1975) *Word Works.* Cambridge: CUP.

Brandreth, G. (1986) *Everyman's Word Games.* London: Dent.

Bunting, R. (1999) *Teaching about Language in the Primary Years.* London: David Fulton Publishers.

Casey, R. and Koshy, V. (1995) *Bright Challenge.* Cheltenham: Stanley Thornes.

Coles, M. J. and Robinson, W. D. (1991) *Teaching Thinking: A Survey of Programmes in Education.* Bristol: Classical Press.

De Bono, E. (1995) *Mind Pack.* London: Dorling Kindersley.

Fisher, R. (1999) *Stories/Games/Poems for Thinking.* Oxford: Nash Pollock Publishing.

Foley, J. (1993) *The Guinness Encyclopaedia of Signs and Symbols.* London: Guinness Publishing.

Griffiths, N. (1997) *Storysacks: a starter information pack.* Swindon: National Storysack Support Project.

Lee, W. R. (1979) *Language Teaching Games and Contests.* Oxford: OUP.

Mensa (1995) *Riddles and Conundrums.* London: Carlton.

Morris, H. (1994) *The New Where's that Poem?* Cheltenham: Stanley Thornes.

Phinn, G. (1995) *Touches of Beauty – teaching poetry in the primary school.* Doncaster: Roselea Publications.

Pike, G. and Selby, D. (1995) *Reconnecting from National to Global Curriculum. (Chapter 4 – English)* Swindon: World Wildlife Fund.

Revell, J. and Norman, S. (1999) *Handing Over – NLP-based activities for language learning.* Sheffield: Saffire Press.

Scher, A. and Verrall, C. (1975) *100+ Ideas for Drama.* London: Heinemann.

Seely, J. (2000) *The Language Kit, Levels 1, 2, 3.* London: Heinemann.

Teare, B. (1999) *Effective Resources Provision for Able and Talented Children.* Stafford: Network Educational Press.

Thomas, R. and Perry, A. (1984) *Into Books.* Oxford: OUP.

Whitely, R. (1995) *Letters Play.* London: Robson Books.

Wray, D. and Lewis, M. (1999) *Non-fiction Writing.* London: Scholastic.

Young Book Trust (1995) *Looking for an Author? A Directory of Authors, Illustrators and Poets.* Reading and Language Information Centre, University of Reading.

Children's books

Blake, Q. (1995) *Clown.* London: Jonathan Cape.

McKewan, I. and Innocenti, R. (1985) *Rose Blanche.* London: Jonathan Cape.

Noon, S. (1998) *A Street through Time.* London: Dorling Kindersley.

Oakley, G. (1986) *Henry's Quest.* London: Macmillan.

Sendak, M. (1992) *Where the Wild Things Are.* London: Harper Collins.

Useful organisations

Poetry Society, 22 Betterton Street, London, WC2H 9BU.

Reading and Language Information Centre, Bulmershe Court, Earley, Reading, RG6 1HY.

Young Book Trust, Book House, 45 East Hill, London, SW18 2QZ.

Young Book Trust, The Scottish Book Centre, 137 Dundee Street, Edinburgh, EH11 1BG.

Useful websites

www.education.bl.uk: The British Library website, which offers free admission, workshops, teachers' packs and website projects.

www.nate.org.uk: National Association of Teachers in English

www.poetryclass.net: A DfEE/Poetry Society initiative for teachers' advice and information on teaching poetry across all key stages.

www.standards.dfee.gov.uk/literacy/glossary. The main NLS website where the glossary of Grammar for Writing is located. Able children could discover a great deal about language from this site.

www.teachit.co.uk: an online library for secondary/English teachers which offer free access to more than 350 photocopiable and downloadable materials.

www.thrass.com: THRASS

encarta.msn.com/LanguageChoice.asp: Encarta Online

www.ngfl.gov.uk: National Grid for Learning

www.vtc.ngfl.gov.uk: Virtual Teachers' Centre

www.vtc.ngfl.gov.uk/resource/literacy/index.html: Literacy Time

www.standards.dfee.gov.uk: DfEE Standards Unit

www.literacytrust.org.uk: The Literacy Trust

www.reading.org: International Reading Association

www.schools.ash.org.au/litweb: Literacy Web (Australia)

www.acs.ucalgary.ca/~dkbrown/index.html: Children's Literature Web Guide (Canada)

www.ed.uri.edu/smart/HOMEPAGE/lithp.html: Literacy Links

www.jetlink.net/~massij/shakes: The Shakespeare Classroom (US)

www.mustang.coled.umn.edu: Language Arts Educators' Jump Page

(Acknowledgements to UKRA and Maureen Lewis for some of the sites listed above.)

CHAPTER 3

Mathematics

Lynne McClure

Introduction

In the introductory chapter we have discussed the need for appropriate provision for able pupils. The issues considered apply equally to mathematics lessons or the daily numeracy session, and in this chapter we shall be answering some of the most frequently asked questions about meeting the needs of the most able in the primary mathematics classroom. We will look at what we mean when we say a child is able in mathematics and how we can tell which children are particularly gifted. We shall then consider ways of meeting those pupils' needs within the typical class, and look at enrichment possibilities outside school. Suggestions for resources including information and communication technology (ICT) are included.

Teachers' perceptions

From my own work with practising and beginning teachers, it seems that certain areas of the primary curriculum affect the confidence levels of teachers differently. The three areas that seem to be the most problematic to the generalist teacher are mathematics, science and music. There appears to be something mystical about the abilities of the gifted pupils in these curriculum areas which causes anxiety to non-specialist teachers. Those practitioners who are not very confident in their own knowledge, skills and understanding in these areas often feel threatened by the outstanding abilities of some of their pupils, or worry that they themselves do not have enough expertise to be able to address their gifted pupils' needs. In some cases this is translated into a reluctance to consider the needs of the able pupil at all. Indeed, some teachers may feel that pupils who are succeeding well at the most difficult parts of the curriculum do not need further stimulation. In this chapter I hope to convince you that the needs of the able mathematician in your class are as important as the needs of any other child, and that you do not need to be an 'expert' yourself in order to meet them.

What do we mean when we describe a child as being able in mathematics?

How might a child be defined as able in maths? Trafton (1981) suggests that there are three groups of pupils who can be described as 'mathematically able'; those who:

- learn content well and perform accurately but find difficulty when taught at a faster pace or at a deeper conceptual level;
- learn more content and at a deeper level, reason well, are capable of solving more complex problems than the average student;
- are highly talented or precocious because they work at the level of a student several years older and seem to need little or no formal instruction. They learn at a faster rate and deal well with sophisticated content and problems.

These three types could conveniently be called more able, most able and exceptionally able although these are not discrete categories. Indeed, most writers (e.g. Kennard 1996, Krutetskii 1976) prefer to consider mathematical ableness as a selection of particular characteristics drawn from a wide menu. The particular recipe of characteristics differs from individual to individual. Another model others have used is a continuum ranging from able through to exceptional. Throughout the chapter are case studies of primary aged pupils working in maths. You may wish to consider where you would place them along the continuum (see Figure 3.1).

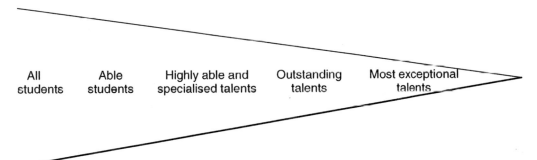

| All students | Able students | Highly able and specialised talents | Outstanding talents | Most exceptional talents |

Figure 3.1 Continuum of ability

Ability changes over time

One of the things we know about primary children is that their abilities change and are expressed differently over time. Identifying able mathematicians at 5 is different from identifying them at say 11, partly because they have fewer skills to exhibit their abilities and partly because their abilities may change. The child who is extremely good at oral number work at 5 may perhaps be benefiting from much parental involvement. The difference between him and his peers may not be sustained when his peers have had a chance to catch up with him.

However, Bloom's three phases of giftedness, described in detail in the first chapter, can be recognised in children of mathematical ability. A broad framework into which researchers have attempted to insert more detail is provided by the three phases of early years' fascination with order and pattern which develops into mastery and subsequently into creative activity. Let us now consider some of the detail.

The early years

Straker (1983) suggested that in the early years, potential can be identified by:

- a liking for numbers including using them in stories and rhymes;
- an ability to argue, question and reason using logical connectives: if, so, because . . .;
- pattern-making revealing balance or symmetry;
- precision in setting out toys, e.g. cars arranged in rows, dolls ordered according to size;
- use of sophisticated criteria for sorting and classification;
- pleasure in jigsaws and other constructional toys.

These characteristics include little in the way of recording. As children get older, the way in which they express their ability may include the way they write about their work, although as we shall see later, there are very able mathematicians of all ages who find it difficult to express themselves verbally, either on paper or in the spoken word.

Older pupils

The Russian, Krutetskii (1976), was one of the first researchers to analyse the methods of working of pupils who had been identified as mathematically able. He suggested that older able mathematicians can:

- grasp the formal structure of a problem in a way that leads to ideas for action;
- generalise from a study of examples;
- reason in a logical way and as a consequence develop chains of reasoning;
- use mathematical symbols and the language of mathematics;
- think flexibly: adapt their ways of approaching problems and switch from one mode of thought to another;
- reverse their direction of thought, work backwards and forwards in an attempt to solve a problem;
- leave out intermediate steps in a logical argument and think in abbreviated mathematical forms;
- remember generalised mathematical relationships, problem types, generalised ways of approaching problems and patterns of reasoning.

Krutetskii also described the ability of able mathematicians to see mathematics all around them in a variety of situations; he called it a 'mathematical turn of mind'. Such children would, for example, recognise or seek symmetry in pattern even where that pattern was nothing to do with formal mathematics, or they might notice number patterns in registration plates of cars. He also described how very able children would persevere at a piece of mathematics long after their peers had lost interest.

Able pupils and the National Numeracy Strategy

In an analysis of able pupils working within the daily numeracy session, the Excellence in Cities national training programme (DfEE 2000) adds that able mathematicians frequently:

- are enthusiastic about and enjoy discussing mathematics, both abstract and concrete;
- show an ability to estimate and predict accurately;
- show persistence and flexibility in their search for solutions;
- apply the same useful approaches to problem solving across a range of contexts;
- perceive the practical and everyday applications of mathematics;
- are able to describe, explain and justify the methods they use;
- may have strengths in different areas of maths;
- are 'holistic' in their approaches to problems, e.g. not necessarily showing exceptional ability with calculations but having an awareness of problems as a whole, or the importance of their choice of processes.

This last characteristic is one upon which several other writers have commented (Koshy 2001). The numeracy strategy emphasises fluency and accuracy in mental and written calculation. Some very able pupils may be unexceptional in this area, preferring to work on the 'bigger picture'. Assessment procedures such as SATs contribute to the identification of competent mathematicians who may be content when addressing computational activities, but become unsettled by anything which requires thinking about maths in a different way. On the other hand, children may not be identified as anything other than very competent unless they are provided with additional opportunities to work at mathematics at a deeper and more complex level. It is unlikely that pupils will exhibit talent in, for example, describing, explaining and justifying their choice of method if they are not given the opportunity to do so. Similarly, small children who are told how to sort their toys may not exhibit the exceptional ability they would have shown had they been allowed to choose their own criteria for sorting. Teachers also need to be aware that high mathematical ability may be masked by a lack of ability in recording or presentation skills, in verbalising or in working cooperatively. We shall discuss this again later (see Figure 3.2).

David (10) scored Level 5 on his KS2 SATs. He was an avid reader and enjoyed creative writing. He excelled at mental arithmetic, having a good memory and the ability to use known facts in a new situation. He disliked repetitious activities and became bored easily if he didn't perceive them as challenging. He would record his work as the writing itself frequently helped him to solve a problem. He often brought mathematical games or activities from home and enjoyed describing and explaining them at show and tell time.

Figure 3.2 Case study 1

How can I recognise able mathematicians?

If able children are identified and then offered different opportunities from everyone else, their experience becomes exclusive. This is Freeman's 'diagnose and treat model' referred to in the introductory chapter. So the child who is identified as an able mathematician and is provided with perhaps the next text book in the maths scheme to work through, or a book of maths challenges to attempt, is not able to share his/her experiences with his/her peers. At the same time, those children who *might* be capable of doing that work are not offered the opportunity. We stated above that identification is usually only possible if appropriate opportunities are provided. Joan Freeman (1998) calls this the 'sports model' approach, because she likens it to not knowing how high a child can jump unless the bar is offered at progressively increased heights. Saying that a child of 7 can meet the level descriptors for Level 2 and therefore does not need to be provided with anything further, is to not 'raise the bar'.

Let us now consider examples of the sort of activities we need to provide so that some of the characteristics of able mathematicians might be exhibited.

Characteristic	Identification opportunity
• pattern-making revealing balance or symmetry • precision in setting out toys, e.g. cars arranged in rows, dolls ordered according to size	Free play with attribute blocks etc. Why did you . . .? Free play, perhaps with open ended activity. Why did you . . .?
• use of sophisticated criteria for sorting and classification	How are these the same/different . . .?
• are enthusiastic about and enjoy discussing mathematics, both abstract and concrete • an ability to argue, question and reason using logical connectives: if, so, because . . . • are able to describe, explain and justify the methods they use	Plenary session or teacher-pupil dialogue. What did you enjoy about . . .?. Why did you . . .?
• show an ability to estimate and predict accurately	In calculations: opportunities to show an awareness of magnitude. In problem solving: opportunities to predict outcomes.
• show persistence and flexibility in their search for solutions	Needs extended time to follow own ideas.
• apply the same useful approaches to problem solving across a range of contexts • perceive the practical and everyday applications of mathematics	Opportunities to tackle problems which have the same underlying structure, e.g. listing all possible variations. Opportunities to solve real problems rather than contrived.
• may have strengths in different areas of maths	Access to whole of the curriculum even if not very able in one part (e.g. not restricted to consolidating number work when others have moved on to shape and space).

• are 'holistic' in their approaches to problems, e.g. not necessarily showing exceptional ability with calculations but having an awareness of problems as a whole, or the importance of their choice of processes	Opportunities to use calculators/computers to do the computation so that the 'bigger picture' can be accessed.
• grasp the formal structure of a problem in a way that leads to ideas for action • reason in a logical way and as a consequence develop chains of reasoning	Opportunities to consider multi dimensional activities that require 'layers' of thinking.
• generalise from a study of examples	Opportunities to look for a rule and express it in their own terms.
• think flexibly: adapt their ways of approaching problems and switch from one mode of thought to another • reverse their direction of thought; work backwards and forwards in an attempt to solve a problem • leave out intermediate steps in a logical argument and think in abbreviated mathematical forms • remember generalised mathematical relationships, problem types, generalised ways of approaching problems and patterns of reasoning	Opportunities for open ended and extended problem solving. Encouragement to record thinking process rather than outcomes. Opportunities to talk about their 'thinking in progress'. Opportunities to record and present work in a variety of ways: e.g. word processed, diagrammatically, orally, recorded onto tape.

Figure 3.3 Opportunities for identification

Other methods of identification

There are of course other methods of identification which may provide a starting point. Previous teachers' reports, baseline assessment, SATs scores, NFER tests and other testing procedures will give an indication of achievement. Asking parents to describe their children's interests will sometimes highlight an area of a child's expertise which can be capitalised upon; for example, the child who delights in logic puzzles or seeks answers to mathematical questions at home. Asking the peer group will also often provide illuminating answers, as will asking the children themselves.

Able underachievers in mathematics

Some very able children underachieve in many areas of the school curriculum, often because of external factors which are outside the control of the school or the teacher. Koshy, for example, describes working in schools with high levels of social deprivation and the effects this can have on children's performance overall (Koshy 2001). But here we shall confine ourselves to looking at those who underachieve in mathematics.

The importance of classroom climate and teacher expectation

One of the things that we know about primary children especially, is that generally they aim to get right answers and please teachers. Thus the ethos of the classroom, where it is acceptable to make mistakes, consider others' points of view and take

Sarah (10) scored Level 5 on her KS2 SATs. Her written work was outstandingly well presented. She enjoyed producing a finished product which was pleasing to the eye. She always scored high marks in mental arithmetic tests and easily remembered mathematical terminology and facts. She enjoyed repetitive work. As long as the work she was given resembled something she had seen previously she was happy. When presented with an unfamiliar problem she required teacher intervention to help her to 'get started' and would require reassurance that she was 'doing it right'. In group situations she was popular because she could be relied upon to do the finishing off.

Figure 3.4 Case study 2

risks, is a very important factor. Research (Coates *et al.* 2001) indicates that successful teachers of able pupils ensure a nurturing classroom climate in which it is safe to take intellectual risks. In such mathematics classrooms pupils are encouraged to evaluate their own work and operate as independent learners; they are provided with opportunities for additional responsibility. Underachievers may be those who, perhaps because of low self-esteem, do not risk failure and therefore set their own sights too low. Or they may be those who, in a non-risk taking classroom, switch off because the subject matter is insufficiently challenging. Intrinsic motivation, according to Deci (in Montgomery 2001), is fostered by 'a consistent, positive, supportive climate and positive constructive feedback. It is destroyed under a pressure to reach and maintain "standards", a fate often assigned to many gifted children. When pupils are exposed to extrinsic motivation, and have to be made to learn, they lose autonomy and self regulation'. Perhaps exhorting our able mathematicians to achieve Level 6 does not always serve them well.

In some schools it is not 'cool' to be bright, and achievement is not celebrated. Able mathematicians may wish to conceal their abilities because of the need to maintain credibilty or 'street cred'. Children who excel in mathematics are often called 'nerds' by their peers. In a recent analysis of pupils' impressions of mathematics teachers, 11 and 12 year olds said:

Mathematicians have no friends, except other mathematicians, not married or seeing anyone, usually fat, very unstylish, wrinkles in their forehead from thinking so hard, no social life whatsoever, 30 years old, a very short temper. (Centre for Teaching Mathematics, Plymouth University, reported in The Times 3 January 2001)

Not a complimentary picture, and one with which few children would wish to be identified!

A mismatch across the curriculum

Underachievers are defined as those for whom attainment does not match potential. This begs the question that there is some way of identifying mathematical potential. Previous results in SATs or other standardised tests might indicate a dip in attainment over time, but a child who has been underachieving continually is more difficult to spot. Where there are discrepancies between for example literacy and oracy, then a test which minimises linguistic and cultural biases such as Raven's Progressive Matrices may help to give a clearer picture.

Underachievers are difficult to identify because by definition they do not have high quality work to show. In mathematics, underachieving children may be identified by looking for those whose profile is irregular, for example those who are good verbally but not good at recording, or those who do not read well and so have problems in accessing written material. Similarly, those for whom English is an additional language may be mathematically gifted but have problems in accessing information or expressing themselves. And teachers who work with pupils whose special needs may disguise their abilities in mathematics should beware that 'the disability is given more attention than the ability, and expectations of what the child will achieve are reduced' (Eyre and Fitzpatrick 2000). There are several well rehearsed checklists for underachievement (such as those summarised in the introductory chapter), of which some are more or less appropriate to use in mathematics.

What can the teacher do to combat underachievement?

In some cases specific help is required in order to ensure access to the curriculum, for example, perhaps providing questions aurally rather than written for those with poor reading skills or offering larger print to those who are visually impaired. As we said above, able children do not fall into distinct categories. Children may be able in some aspect of maths, number work for example, but be fairly average at work in shape and space, and vice versa. So if we offer different maths experiences only to a predetermined group of able children, we run the risk of missing those who may be particularly good at only one particular area. Ensuring that all pupils have access to the more challenging parts of the maths curriculum could identify those who have particular ability.

Ben (10) scored Level 4 on KS2 SATs. He had great problems in recording his work. Mostly he didn't see the need for it because he could think much quicker than he could write. His handwriting was barely legible and his spelling poor. He would avoid writing anything down at all wherever possible. He disliked mental arithmetic because he was not very fast at it and had difficulty remembering, for example, his times tables. He could, however, work the answers out using his own methods which were often elegant. His strengths lay in the analysis of a problem where he would work forwards and backwards and draw from strategies he had learnt elsewhere. He did not work well in a group as others thought him arrogant and dismissive. His response to the whole school maths challenge 'Show a hundred' was to use a hundred spent matches to form the symbols for a very long sum, the answer to which was exactly a hundred.

Figure 3.5 Case study 3

What maths to teach and how to teach it

Assuming then that we have identified those who are gifted and achieving in mathematics, and have an idea which of our pupils are underachieving, how best can we then meet those children's needs within the school and classroom context?

Written guidance to date says that teachers will need to plan 'suitably challenging' work for the able pupils in their mathematics class (National Curriculum DfEE 1999). The new National Curriculum documentation also suggests that as well as drawing on materials from later key stages or higher levels of study, teachers may plan further differentiation by extending the breadth and depth of study within individual subjects or by planning work that draws on the content of different subjects. The National Numeracy Strategy specific guidance has already been written and there is more to come (DfEE 2000). The National Curriculum guidance offers three alternatives in the way in which the learning objectives could be covered:

- at a faster pace;
- to a broader range;
- in greater depth.

We shall now look at each of these options, considering the implications for the child, the teacher and school/class organisation.

Working at a faster pace

This means moving through the same work as everyone else but faster. We can see this in schools where the able pupils work through the text books of a maths scheme quicker than the majority of the class. They may do this individually, in a group within a mixed ability class, or as a set where the school is large enough to set by ability for this subject. In small primary schools where classes span a two-year, or sometimes three-year age range, able mathematicians are sometimes offered the same curriculum as their older classmates. In other schools where the timetable allows, the able mathematicians move during mathematics lessons to classes of older pupils. In extreme cases, children move across key stages and even to different institutions.

Implications for the pupil

Solutions such as these are based on the assumption that the 'normal' curriculum provides what the able student needs. It offers able pupils no more mathematics than those who struggle with the subject, but only the same mathematics, sooner. While the National Curriculum for mathematics sets out the statutory entitlement for all pupils, it is possible to think of it as a minimum entitlement for those who have particular mathematical talents and who would benefit from, and enjoy learning about, the diversity and wealth of mathematics.

Younger talented pupils may, perhaps, be socially immature compared to the children in the class above. They may be resented by the peers in their own class because of moving to a different class. Social tensions may mean that group work may not be as productive as it might be. When pupils move into higher classes to work with older pupils, they may be covering the same content as them but may not be working with pupils of the same intellectual calibre. Working collaboratively with averagely talented peers may mean that the quality of interaction is less stimulating. We know that able pupils enjoy working with like minded peers (Kennard 1996) and benefit from such collaboration.

And again there is a great temptation that because able mathematicians are frequently (though not always) good readers, self-motivated and sometimes well-behaved, work of this sort can be seen as something to 'get on with'. It is not unusual for able children to report remembering very little teaching and commenting that most of their maths, especially at primary school, was self-taught. Exceptionally able pupils can sometimes feel very lonely when they have to plough through material by themselves. Able mathematicians, like everyone else, are entitled to teaching and monitoring, not merely being organised.

Implications for the teacher

Joan Freeman describes acceleration as the 'cheapest, easiest and most usual form of special provision' (Freeman 1998). For the teacher, it can be the easiest option as it usually involves using available resources such as the next book or stage in a scheme. Apart from the organisational difficulties, which are common to all forms of individual or group work, generally acceleration creates less work for the individual teacher. A possible advantage of working quickly through a content-based curriculum is the effect on SATs results. Key Stage 1 pupils might attain Level 3 or 4, and 11 year olds achieve Level 5 or even Level 6 if they have had access to the content of the Level 6 programme of study. We have already mentioned the possible negative effects on the child of pressure to attain externally imposed standards. In addition, acceleration may also be a short-term solution, because once a pupil has been accelerated through part of the curriculum, that offered in the succeeding years will need to be adjusted too, either by the same teacher in a mixed age class, or by the teacher of the next one.

In the recently published paper 'Acceleration or enrichment?' (UK Maths Foundation 2000) the case for acceleration in mathematics, at all ages, is discussed. The writers suggest that two crucial conditions should be met in order for acceleration to be a successful strategy for the child in the long term.

1. Children should have complete mastery of the mathematics curriculum appropriate for their age before they are allowed to accelerate, and
2. there should be a coherent school policy to ensure that continuity of provision is ensured.

The mathematics education community strongly recommend that only if both conditions are met fully should acceleration be considered as an appropriate form of provision for able mathematicians. Despite all of these disdvantages there are, of course, pupils for whom acceleration works exceptionally well. We will return to individuals' needs later.

Working at greater depth

This means able pupils working within the same topic area as the rest of the class but undertaking activities which extend the sort of thinking required. Many lessons in mathematics, and especially those involving number work, include activities which focus on what Bloom denoted as 'lower order thinking skills' of knowledge and comprehension (Appendix One). Examples of these kinds of activities would be those involving recall (such as testing number bonds, multiplication tables, knowing the connection between different units of measures) explaining what they recall (carrying out an algorithm, continuing a number pattern etc.) or applying their knowledge to simple problems. Able pupils are often very efficient at these kinds of activities and quickly become bored by doing 'more of the same'.

However most pupils, but particularly able pupils, will benefit from extending the same topic into activities which promote the higher order thinking skills of analysis, evaluation and synthesis. Investigations can be extended by setting able pupils additional or alternative objectives such as predicting the outcome, finding a rule and explaining why it works or to prove it, hypothesising (what would happen if) or choosing a different method of recording and presenting their findings. Other activities could include asking pupils to look for a quicker or more elegant way of doing the same problem, and evaluating their own strategies or approaches. While *all* pupils can benefit from discussing how they began work on a problem or what approaches were the most successful, more able pupils by their very nature are often even better placed to profit from talking about the way they approach tasks. In this respect the teacher, by modelling and making explicit the strategies used, can benefit able pupils especially.

In order to allow extra time for this work, it may be appropriate to compact the curriculum for able pupils who do not need to consolidate lower level skills, in order to give time for them to work at higher levels. It may also be appropriate for an exceptionally able child who needs to learn a new skill (in order to be able to apply it to either of the categories above), to be offered some of the work of students a year or so older.

Implications for the pupil

Teachers very often find the whole-class activities (the introduction and plenary) of the tripartite numeracy lesson model the most difficult to manage, because of the wide ability range which must be taken into account. From the pupils' point of view, however, alternatives or extensions to the main focus of a whole-class lesson within the same mathematical area allow them to share their work and take part in whole-class activities. Activities such as these can therefore work well within the primary numeracy lesson framework because they make the whole-class introduction and plenary relevant for all the members of the class. Whole class discussions of strategies used by the more able children may also allow less able pupils to experience the way of working of their more able peers, and they may perhaps remember some of those strategies the next time they work on a similar problem.

Pupils who are very competent in one area of the curriculum can work on higher order tasks while remaining with the rest of the class in working in other areas in which they may not be so successful. In this way the pupil is not locked into extension activities as a matter of course, but can be selected (or opt in themselves) when it is appropriate for them to do so. The curriculum for the most able then begins to become inclusive rather than exclusive. Activities planned across a variety of mathematical topics but with the same elements can enable pupils to recognise a similar underlying structure and possible common strategies for solution.

Implications for the teacher

Providing opportunities for pupils to work at a deeper level is possibly the most difficult strategy for teachers who are not very confident in their own mathematical ability. However, within the climate of an enquiring classroom it is not necessary for the teacher to know the answer to all problems or investigations – the 'I don't know, let's find out' approach is one which able pupils especially enjoy. The important issue is that the teacher needs to be aware of what 'greater depth' means in the mathematical context, as well as the appropriate vocabulary to use with the children.

In the first instance, activities promoting higher order thinking need to be planned. Medium-term and short-term plans could include a section where detailed information about appropriate activities is recorded, including the type of questions which may elicit higher order thinking. We know that the type of questions that teachers ask has a profound effect on the type of learning that takes place (Kerry and Kerry 2000). Questions that require factual answers encourage retrieval of knowledge, and comprehension. Questions of the how and why variety encourage application, synthesis, analysis and evaluation. In the following chapter about science in the primary curriculum, you can read in more detail about the importance of asking the right questions. There are many similarities between science and mathematics in this respect.

Some published schemes now include these types of activities in their teachers' resource books. Teachers who have written medium-term lesson plans to include such activity report that they become progressively more aware of many opportunities to introduce questions leading to sophisticated thinking on the part of *all* their pupils (Coates *et al.* 2001). In many cases the responses from pupils not previously identified as being particularly able lead the teacher to reassess the pupils. I referred to this cyclical nature of provision and identification above – children can only show how able they are if they are given the opportunity to do so.

What does this mean in practice?

Year group	Learning outcome of activity	Description of activity
Year 2	**Class activity:** NNS; Describe and identify common 3-d shapes accurately, according to their properties.	Group activity: Each group has a selection of 3-d shapes in the centre of the table. The children take turns to be the guesser and turn away while the rest of the group secretly and together agree on one of the shapes. They group then take turns around the table to give one piece of information about the chosen shape and the guesser tries to identify which shape they are thinking about.
	Extension activity: This activity refines the thinking of the whole-class activity and requires the children to analyse the characteristics of each shape. Using a flow chart requires them to synthesise the information from all the shapes, and the competitive element ensures evaluation of the usefulness of each question.	Group or individual activity. The group has a similar set of 3-d shapes as above (12 is ideal). They sort them in as many ways possible and then each child devises a series of yes/no questions which when answered will enable them to identify each shape. They try these out on each other. The challenge is to devise as few different questions as possible.

Figure 3.6 Working at a deeper level at KS 1

Year group	Learning outcome of activity	Description of activity
Year 4	**Class of activity** NNS; Use number facts and place value to add or subtract mentally, including any pair of two-digit numbers. This activity requires participants to operate at the knowledge and comprehension levels of Bloom's taxonomy.	This is a paired activity intended for the main part of the numeracy session. In turn partners use throws of a 0–9 dice (or a random selection from 0–9 cards) to determine the integer values of two two-digit numbers, which are then recorded. Both partners add their two numbers mentally and the answer is checked and agreed by both. Whoever has the larger answer collects the difference between the two answers (calculated mentally and agreed again) and records it. After 5 rounds the winner is the partner with the larger total.
		A B 3 4 0 9 5 2 + 7 1 + _____ _____ 8 6 8 0
		Partner A has won round 1 and so collects 6 points which is the difference between 86 and 80.
	Extension activity: Evaluate the difficulty of two-digit addition and subtraction calculations. This activity requires the children to *analyse* the steps in the calculation and *evaluate* the difficulty analysis and evaluation. (Bloom)	In pairs, the children are given a list of addition or subtraction calculations involving two two-digit numbers. They discuss how they would calculate the answers and then rank the questions in order of difficulty, justifying their decisions. They could then generate their own graded series of examples for their peers.

Figure 3.7 Working at a deeper level at KS2

Working within a broader range

Offering activities within a broader range does not mean doing harder examples of the same kind of task. Enriching and broadening the range of the maths on offer means doing maths outside the prescribed curriculum and making connections with other curriculum areas. The most obvious activities are those included in investigation or puzzle books of which there are an increasing number available. But enrichment could be focused around a centre of interest set up to encourage pupils to explore, for example, an historical aspect of mathematics, or to investigate a particular piece of maths equipment such as a clinometer. A visit from an adult with particular expertise could be the starting point for a project which pupils could then present to their peers. The 'free time' within the numeracy strategy timetable could provide an opportunity for personal research such as this, which ideally requires an extended period of time.

Implications for the pupil

Mathematically exceptionally able pupils very often have areas of the curriculum which they find particularly attractive. Being allowed the time and resources to pursue an area such as this in greater depth can be very fulfilling for the child, especially if time and attention is given for the presentation of the findings to the peer group. If given as homework, teachers must ensure that resources are available at home for personal research. Puzzles and problem sheets, on the other hand, can often be perceived by pupils as unrelated to the rest of the curriculum and care needs to be taken in the choice of such resources.

Implications for the teacher

Enrichment activities such as these are relatively easy for the teacher to plan into the daily maths lesson. There is a wide range of printed and on-line resources available to support the teacher of any age class. But unless there are clear aims they can easily be time-fillers with little worth other than of general interest. As with the previously described activities, enrichment activities should not be opportunities for pupils to be left to investigate alone; able mathematicians are entitled to teacher time and expertise as much as the lower-attaining pupils in the class. It is helpful if the objectives are shared with the pupils too: finding out as much as you can about Pythagoras can be especially daunting for an able 11 year old who has an appreciation of how far-reaching such an investigation could be!

What does this mean in practice?

Year group	Learning outcome of activity	Description of activity
Year 1	**Class activity:** NNS; Understand that more than two numbers can be added together.	Individual activity. Using a worksheet and a number line, pupils explore the different ways of making three hops to 15. They fill in $6 \ + \ 5 \ + \ \square \ = 15$ $4 \ + \ 7 \ + \ \square \ = 15$ etc.
	Broader activity: Ensuring that puzzles are part of the topic being undertaken by the whole class can be tricky. Here the children are consolidating their number skills then considering alternative solutions. Using number cards to help reduces the need for a lot of rubbing out.	Individual activity. Pupils use their 1–9 cards to help them to fill in magic squares, in which all the rows columns and diagonals add up to 15 (or another number). The squares are graded, getting progressively more difficult by requiring more numbers to be filled in. Children who succeed easily at this could explore different ways of beginning with an empty number square, or choosing a different total. <table><tr><td>4</td><td>9</td><td>2</td></tr><tr><td></td><td>5</td><td>7</td></tr><tr><td>8</td><td></td><td></td></tr></table>

Figure 3.8 Broadening the experience at KS 1

Year group	Learning outcome of activity	Description of activity
Year 6	**Class activity:** NNS; recognise reflective symmetry in 2-d shapes, reflections and translations.	Individual activity: Generate patterns having two lines of symmetry by sketching the reflection of a shape in two mirror lines at right angles.
	Broader activity: Independent research to collect and analyse artefacts from other cultures for reflective symmetry.	Group or individual activity. Use books and on-line resources to find examples of symmetry in art from other cultures. Make a presentation in a medium of own choice. Pupils who have no difficulty with the concept of line symmetry find doing more examples of the same tedious. Collecting together intercultural (and including historical) examples, with descriptions of the kind of symmetry they display, can inform the rest of the class too. Rangoli patterns are a good starter.

Figure 3.9 Broadening the experience at KS2

The exceptionally able

If we return to the continuum of ability described at the beginning of this chapter we can see that there will occasionally be an exceptionally able mathematician whose needs we cannot meet in the normal classroom situation. Such children deserve specialised provision and an individual education plan. The role of the classroom teacher, together with the maths coordinator, gifted and talented coordinator and parents, is to recognise the talent and facilitate a programme of study which may include mentoring, or perhaps attendance at a different institution (secondary school or university).

While considering the child's intellectual ability, the social and emotional needs must also be taken into account. Work undertaken by Van Tassel-Baska (1985) and others, indicate that mathematics is one of those areas where acceleration is an effective and economic way of developing talent for the exceptionally able.

It may be that a mentor enables the child to accelerate through the curriculum through specialised teaching at an advanced level and perhaps public examinations may be taken ahead of the peer group. Or a mentor may provide enrichment activities outside the recognised curriculum which would require the child to work at greater depth in areas of interest. As with all children, it is important that there must not be a 'quick fix'. Before embarking on a radical change, continuity and progression must be discussed and planned for. Just as each gifted child is individual, so there is no best course of action for the exceptionally talented.

Adam (4) always chose to play independently and with collections of toys or apparatus. He would organise and reorganise the farm animals, cars, building blocks, Lego etc, seeming to prefer their underlying characteristics than the opportunity they afforded for imaginative play. He would spend long periods of time writing 'sums' and liked to be asked questions about numbers, especially big ones. He was fascinated by nought, could count backwards with ease and developed his own names for negative numbers, calling them 'not one not two' etc.

Figure 3.10 Case study 4

Organisational strategies

Setting

Most primary teachers teach large, mixed ability classes for most subjects. In recent years schools with sufficiently large numbers have set their pupils by ability, especially at the top of the school, for mathematics (Sukhandan and Lee 1998). Parents of gifted pupils are more likely to choose schools that implement ability grouping than those which do not (Gewirtz, Ball and Bowe 1995). The numeracy strategy guidance states that one advantage of such arrangements is that planning for a narrower ability band can be easier. However, as we have read in the introductory chapter, setting does not in itself ensure appropriate provision. Very often there is a larger ability range in the top set than in the lowest, and consideration must be given to differentiation within a set as well as between them. OFSTED reported that even in those schools which used ability setting, the match of work was poor in a third of lessons, failing to take account of the range of ability within each set (OFSTED 1994).

Setting works best where movement between sets is fluid. In primary schools the timetable usually allows children to move from one set to another, but research shows that pupils rarely move across sets and that they perform according to which set they are assigned to (Hallam and Toutounji 1996). The same research indicates that pupils are placed in maths sets not only according to their ability. Many top sets contain quiet, well-behaved and tidy girls while rowdy, non-conforming boys are very often placed in the lower sets.

Ability grouping within classes

Setting is not the only option. Some schools retain mixed ability teaching in the numeracy session although they combine it with within-class grouping. There is research to indicate that within-class grouping in maths increases pupil achievement for all pupils (Harlen and Malcolm 1997) while findings concerning the effects of setting on achievement were inconclusive (Slavin 1987), both to be found in Sukandan and Lee (1998).

Mixed ability

Research indicates that totally mixed ability grouping can have a negative impact on high ability pupils' levels of achievement and motivation (Reid, Clunies, Goacher and Vile 1981). Fielker (1997) however, argues that the setting and ability grouping in maths, prevalent in primary schools, is more for the administrative convenience of the teacher than to meet the needs of the child. He puts forward a convincing argument, and suggests activities, for working with the whole class on problem solving activities for at least part of the time.

What form of organisational strategy you choose to employ will depend on the organisational structure of your school, and its ethos. Edwards and Woodhead (1996) concluded that, for mathematics in the primary school, 'groupings need to be flexibly applied to fitness for purpose incorporating combinations of within-class, group, and individual teaching'.

Resources

Extra resources in themselves do not necessarily improve the learning opportunities of able pupils, the way in which they are used may. However, there are some additional resources that are essential for the more able in your class. In particular, do ensure that your library, or your classroom, has reference materials at an appropriate level for independent study. Most primary classrooms are well stocked with reference materials for the humanities or science but not for mathematics. The content should also be checked for readability levels because, as we have discussed earlier, not all mathematicians are very good readers. A range of maths dictionaries of varying levels of difficulty is useful, too.

When choosing puzzles, problem books or games try to pick those which are very open ended so that they can be used at a variety of different levels. Some published schemes, such as the New Cambridge Primary Maths modules have packs of open-ended games that can be adapted or changed by the players.

ICT can be used as a resource to support mathematics in three distinct ways. The first is as a vast resource bank to supplement written material, just as in other curriculum areas. These resources which are held on the web or CD-Rom are now too numerous to list; there are some useful starter websites which provide both information for independent research as well as activities. Details are at the end of this chapter. The second use of ICT is as tool to enable pupils to consolidate knowledge and/or skills through the use of self-correcting programs, i.e. the computer as tutor. The pupil can work independently through a large number of examples without teacher intervention (or marking). For able mathematicians, programs, such as those in the SMILE suites or individual learning packages such as Successmaker can support them in acquiring quickly a new skill which they may need in order to work at a deeper level. The third use of ICT is as a cognitive teaching tool where particular programs allow the pupil to explore complicated concepts and work at the higher levels of thinking. In the following chapter on ICT, Chris Higgins explores this latter use in depth, but in particular you may wish to rethink your use of spreadsheets, logo-type programs and data handling packages.

'My own mathematics isn't very good'

We have mentioned before the lack of confidence that many primary teachers, who are expected to be experts in all National Curriculum subjects, have in maths. But we have a professional responsibility to ensure that we do not restrict the children in our classes by our own lack of knowledge. Even limited mathematical expertise can be used effectively if there is a willingness to be open to new ideas.

To support your own development in teaching able pupils in maths, you could use the opportunities afforded by demonstration lessons taken by leading mathematics teachers to focus on the teaching and learning of the most able. You may wish to join one of the mathematical associations; research indicates that effective teachers of able pupils themselves portray intellectual curiosity in that subject area. If it is part of your school's appraisal process, you may wish to ask your gifted mathematicians how they think you're doing. You may receive some surprising answers. . .

Itsuka joined the school at 8 with very little English. She had her own methods of written calculation at which she was very practised, and although she was initially understandably slow at mental calculation, when presented orally she could compute much quicker than her peers. She enjoyed the work in 2-d shape and space which required accurate measurement but did not enjoy 3-d activities involving spatial awareness. She preferred to work with a partner.

Figure 3.11 Case study 5

How does all this fit in with the rest of the school?

Meeting the needs of the able children in your class is much easier if there is a whole-school understanding of the needs of the gifted mathematicians. This may be formalised within a whole-school policy or within individual curriculum documents. It may be that you have an informal understanding that has been arrived at by years of close and cooperative work with colleagues, but it is worth considering writing this down somewhere so that new members of staff understand your priorities too.

At the beginning of Key Stage 1, working with preschool providers who may have identified very able young mathematicians will help to ensure that appropriate provision is put in place immediately. You may wish to supplement the baseline assessment with additional questions or tasks which allow small children to show advanced understanding. As able children then move through the school, tracking pupil progress is very important, especially where acceleration may have taken place. This also applies as pupils move from one school to another – able pupils especially look forward to secondary schools and 'real maths' and then frequently find themselves repeating the four rules of number for the first term to 'even out the playing field'. Secondary school colleagues are becoming increasingly aware of the need to build on the experiences that very able pupils have had in primary schools and the initiatives at Key Stage 3 will help them in this. Many clusters of primary schools have developed fruitful relationships with their partner secondary schools which involve exchange visits between staff and joint activities. In Oxfordshire for example, a primary masterclass network is planned, with sessions delivered by primary and secondary colleagues working in partnership.

Challenging the stereotypes of able mathematicians can be achieved through raising the profile of maths throughout the school, for example through whole-school assemblies or involving the whole school in a regular maths challenges (see Figure 3.12). You could enter children for competitions such as the new Primary Maths Challenge which is a national competition run by the Maths Association and UKMT, organised along the same lines as the senior competition. The winners go forward to represent their country at the International Maths Olympiad. Celebrating maths successes in public, including information to parents and displays in prominent areas as well as in your own classroom, can emphasise the 'cool to be bright' message.

Many schools organise out-of-school maths clubs which allow pupils to broaden their experience or to study interest areas in depth. Some are focused on ICT, capitalising on the wealth of maths games on the market. Bringing in experts or communicating on-line with people who have more expertise than you have to offer can also be a focus for these enrichment activities. Nrich, the interactive web site of Cambridge University and the Royal Institution has over 6,000 members worldwide. Among the ever expanding contents are enrichment activities for primary and secondary pupils, ideas for teachers, and the 'Ask a mathematician' service. There is also a mentoring project for extremely able (and sometimes very young) mathematicians. The contact information is included at the end of this chapter.

It might be possible for your able students to take part in mathematics masterclasses offered locally, such as those mentioned above. The Royal Institution has been organising masterclasses in maths and science for many years. There is now a network of secondary maths masterclasses over much of Britain, often

Raising the profile

One way of using the maths challenge is as the focus of a whole-school assembly once a month. At each assembly the entries from the previous challenge are discussed. Choosing one or two entries from each year group or key stage to talk about ensures that the younger children see how the older ones tackled the challenge, and less able competitors benefit from seeing the creativity employed by the most able, too. Prizes may be awarded (pencils printed with an appropriate message are popular) and the winners' work displayed prominently, perhaps in the entrance hall. The new challenge is then introduced. If you use a printed sheet it should have brief instructions or explanation to parents and carers, the date for return and a space for name and class information.

The sort of activities which work best are open-ended ones which can be attempted by children of all ages. One idea is to alternate between number challenges and those involving shape and space in order to attract different groups of children. I have listed a few examples I have used below but the possibilities are many. Another variation is to ask the able pupils to suggest the challenge activity and lead on the introduction. Analysing what is an appropriate challenge for the whole school is a worthwhile activity in itself.

Show a hundred. We did this on the hundredth day of the school year. Entries included early years children bringing a hundred pieces of pasta on a string, various rectangular and square arrays of objects, the word 'HUNDRED' made from a hundred squares and Ben's magnificent effort using a hundred spent matches to form a sum, the answer to which was a hundred.

Colour half. The printed sheet had a large square. Generally the younger children used their energies in colouring while the older ones devised various ways of dividing the square into smaller parts. As an introduction we looked at the SMILE programme 'Take half'.

Explode a number. A target number is written in the middle of the sheet and the competitors make that number in as many unusual ways as possible. More able pupils used calculators to help them to use powers, roots, or three or four step calculations.

The clown. The printed page had the outline of a clown's face. The children were asked to make it symmetrical. Some of the younger children painted or stuck bits of paper to form the face. Some realised that if they cut two pieces from a folded piece of paper their faces 'matched'. Older pupils measured and used pairs of compasses to construct accurate drawings.

Stars. The introductory assembly was used to show a variety of shapes and generate shared understanding of what was a star. Some pupils brought in two dimensional pictures but some of the older more able pupils constructed 3-d stellated polyhedra. The entries made a seasonal display in the entrance hall.

How many eggs? This activity was closed because there is one correct answer. The challenge is a story about a farmer who collected eggs which were large medium or small, brown or white, whole or broken and speckled or plain. The children were asked to draw all the eggs. Younger pupils drew them randomly, older ones were methodical in ensuring they had drawn them all. At the assembly at the end of the challenge we did the activity with large cut-out eggs to determine the minimum number.

Figure 3.12 Maths Challenge

centred at a higher education institution. Able pupils from a group of schools join together to work on mathematics outside their usual curriculum. The recently formed Primary Mathematics Network is following a similar format but the groups in operation to date are usually organised by groups of interested teachers. The Royal Institution can offer financial and organisational support to new groups should you find some other like-minded colleagues.

What else is going on?

There have been several additional outcomes from the Excellence in Cities strategy which particularly affect the mathematics community. QCA have developed world class tests which have been piloted and are now to be introduced in maths and problem solving. They will be available for pupils of Years 9 and 13 and you can find more information about them, and specimen questions, through the QCA website. The DfEE, together with the National Primary Trust, have established Advanced Maths Centres in various parts of the country at present within designated Excellence in Cities areas. To able primary mathematicians they offer a variety of opportunities ranging from enrichment activities to early entry for GCSE.

The Mathematically Promising Network, in conjunction with other subject associations, is in the process of establishing a cross-curricular website called Xcalibre. This will be a directory of provision for able students of all ages, and will have a search facility so that teachers can look up, for example, mathematical events happening in their own area. Maths Year 2000 has been the vehicle for enrichment activities around the UK and many of these are continuing after the official time span. Their website has been widely acclaimed and has a wealth of ideas for enrichment activity. Other organisations such as the Maths Roadshow take travelling mathematics exhibitions and workshops to schools that invite them. The Mathematics Enhancement Programme based at Exeter University also offers support and resources to primary and secondary teachers, as do the subject associations.

Conclusion

Working with able mathematicians can be rewarding and sometimes exciting. It is also a responsibility; they must not be ignored just because they can cope easily with the standard curriculum. Just as every child is different so every teacher is unique, and the way that you interact with each other will not follow a set pattern. However, by picking and mixing the ideas in this chapter, I hope you will meet the challenge of the needs of the gifted children with whom you will come into contact, and that in retrospect they will realise that you were instrumental in guiding them through to greater achievement. Enjoy!!

Useful information

Websites and addresses

ATM Association of Teachers of Mathematics http://www.atm.org.uk

Coolmaths http://www.coolmath.com/American fun maths site

Hoagies gifted and talented site http://www.hoagieskids.org/kidsMnS.htm Americansite with lots of links

MA The Mathematical Association http://www.m-a.org.uk/

Maths Year 2000 http://mathsyear2000.org

MEP Mathematics Enhancement Programme http://www.ex.ac.uk Resources from Exeter University

MPN Mathematically Promising Network http://www.meikleriggs.totalserve.co.uk/mpn

NACE: National Association for Able Children in Education. PO Box 242, Arnold's Way, Oxford OX2 9FR

NAGC: National Association for Gifted Children National Centre for Children with High Abilties and Talents, Elder House, Milton Keynes MK9 1LR

NCTM National Council of Teachers of Mathematics http://www.nctm.org/Very large American organisation with lots of links to gifted and talented sites especially in the USA

NRICH http://nrich.maths.org.uk Online maths enrichment club of Cambridge University. A vast resource for pupils, parents and teachers. Not to be missed!

QCA http://www.qca.org.uk/ information about support material and guidance, and world class tests

RECAP: Research Centre for Able Pupils, Westminster Institute of Education, Oxford Brookes University, Harcourt Hill, Oxford OX2 9AT recap@brookes.ac.uk

RI Royal Institution of Great Britain http://www.ri.ac.uk/ Information about primary maths and science lectures in London and other areas, and masterclass networks

SMILE (1988) Resource Pack. Isaac Newton Centre for Professional Development, Lancaster Road, London W11 1QS.

Xcalibre http://xcalibre.ac.uk Cross-curricular directory of information for gifted and talented

Useful reading

Atkinson, S., Harrison, S. and McClure, L, (1995) *New Cambridge Primary Maths Modules 1 and 2*. Cambridge: Cambridge University Press.

Atkinson, S. (ed.) (1992) *Maths with Reason: The emergent approach to primary maths*. London: Hodder and Stoughton.

DfEE (2000) *Mathematical Challenges for Able Pupils in Key Stages 1 and 2*. London: The Stationery Office.

DfEE (2000) *National literacy and numeracy strategies: Guidance on teaching able children*. London: The Stationery Office.

Edwards, S. (1998) *Managing effective teaching of Mathematics 3–8*. London: Paul Chapman Publishing.

Murray, J. (2000) *Micromaths* 16/2 ATM.

Pennington, E. and Faux, G. (2000) *No Royal Road to Geometry.* Carlisle Education Initiatives.

Ridge, H. L. and Renzulli, J. S. (1981) 'Teaching Mathematics to the Talented and Gifted', In Glennon, V. J. (ed.) *The Mathematical Education of Exceptional Children and Youth.* New York: Creating Learning.

Teare, B. (1997) *Effective Provision for Able and Talented Children.* Stafford: Network Press.

References

Askew, M. and Wiliam, D. (1995) *Recent Research in Mathematics Education 5–16. OFSTED Review of Research.* London: HMSO.

Coates, D. *et al.* (2001 in press) *Expert Teachers of Able Pupils.* Oxford: National Primary Trust.

Cox, B. (1991) *Cox on Cox.* London: Hodder and Stoughton.

DfEE (1999) *The National Curriculum for England: Mathematics, Key Stages 1–4.* London: The Stationery Office

DfEE (2000) *Excellence in Cities.* London: HMSO.

Edwards, S. and Woodhead, N. (1996) 'Mathematics teaching in primary schools: whole class, group or individual teaching?', *Primary Practice*, **6**, 4–7.

Education and Employment Select Committee (1998) *Highly Able Children.* London: HMSO.

Eyre, D. (1997) 'Teaching able pupils', *Support for Learning* 12(2), 60–6 NASEN.

Eyre, D. and Fitzpatrick M. in Benton, P. and O'Brien, P. (eds) (2000) *Special Needs and the Beginning Teacher.* London: Continuium.

Fielker, D. (1997) *Extending Mathematical Ability through Whole Class Teaching.* London: Hodder and Stoughton.

Freeman, J. (1998) *Educating the Very Able. OFSTED.* London: The Stationery Office.

Gewirtz, S., Ball, S. J. and Bowe, R. (1995) *Markets, Choice and Equity in Education.* Buckingham: Open University Press.

Hallam, S. and Toutounji, I. (1996) 'What do we know about grouping pupils by ability?', *Educational Review* **10**(2).

Kennard, R. (1996) *Teaching Mathematically Able Children.* Oxford: NACE.

Kerry, T. and Kerry, C. (2000) 'The centrality of teaching skills in improving able pupil education', *Educating Able Children*, **4**(2), 13–19.

Koshy, V. (2001) *Teaching Mathematics to Able Children.* London: David Fulton Publishers.

Krutetskii, V. A. (1976) *The Psychology of Mathematical Abilities in School Children.* Chicago: University of Chicago Press.

Montgomery, D. (2001) *Able Underachievers.* London: Whurr.

OFSTED (1994) *Primary Matters: A Discussion of Teaching and Learning in Primary Schools.* London: The Stationery Office.

OFSTED (1998) *The Annual Report of Her Majesty's Inspector of Schools: Standards and Quality in Education 1996/97.* London: The Stationery Office.

QCA (2001) *Exemplification Material Supporting Gifted and Talented in Numeracy.* Suffolk: QCA Enterprises Ltd.

QCA (2000) *Guidance on Meeting the Requirements of Gifted and Talented Pupils.* Suffolk: QCA Enterprises Ltd.

RECAP (2000) *Numeracy Strategy Launchpad.* Iley, P. 'Gifted and talented co-ordinators' training Programme', (internal document).

Reid, M. I., Clunies-Ross, L. R., Goacher, B. and Vile, C. (1981) *Mixed Ability Teaching: Problems and Possibilities.* Windsor: NFER-Nelson.

Straker, A. (1983) *Mathematics for Gifted Pupils.* London: Longmans.

Sukandan, L. and Lee, B. (1998) *Streaming, Setting and Grouping by Ability.* Windsor: NFER.

Trafton, P. (1981) 'Overview of providing for mathematically able students', *The Arithmetic Teacher* 28(6), 12–13.

UK Mathematics Foundation (2000) *Acceleration or enrichment?* Birmingham University.

Van Tassel-Baska (1985) 'Acceleration' in Maker, J. (ed.) *Critical issues in Gifted Education.* Rockville MD: Aspen Publications.

CHAPTER 4

Science

David Coates and Helen Wilson

Introduction

When challenging the gifted and talented, it is not always necessary to look towards the amount of work that is done but rather to the cognitive demands that it makes upon children and, in particular, the use of higher order thinking skills. Science is all about thinking and questioning, so it is a subject that is particularly suited to providing such challenge. Sadly, many people's memories of school science are of dry, boring lessons with Bunsen burners or of a potentially elusive search for a 'right' answer in an examination.

Gardner's (1994) study on seven 'creators of the modern era' includes the profound thought that creative individuals are those who see old knowledge in new ways and generate novel ideas or products in their domain. This is eminently true of the heroes of scientific thinking, such as Galileo or Einstein. Scientists need to be able to think creatively and deeply.

Diezmann and Watters (2000) make a comparison between evolutionary thinkers and revolutionary thinkers:

Evolutionary thinkers build on and extend existing ideas and apply those ideas in new ways, while revolutionary thinkers are those creative geniuses who contribute ideas that lead to paradigm shifts (p. 6).

This sums up beautifully the greatest scientists – they are the revolutionary thinkers. They are the ones who have had the courage to break away from the mould of the accepted thinking of their times. For a host of reasons, this type of thinking needs to be encouraged and nurtured. This has been acknowledged in the National Curriculum (DfEE/QCA 1999):

Science stimulates and excites pupils' curiosity about phenomena and events in the world around them. Because science links direct practical experience with ideas, it can engage learners at many levels. Scientific method is about developing and evaluating explanations through experimental evidence and modelling. This is a spur to critical and creative thought. Through science, pupils understand how major scientific ideas contribute to technological change – impacting on industry, business and medicine and improving quality of life (p. 76).

It is salutary to pause and wonder if the weight of the curriculum in the primary school is such that there may be little time for the children to think hard because there is so much work to be done! Science in the primary school can give the children the opportunity to extend their thought processes in some depth. We believe that it is possible to challenge children within science using the normal curriculum and activities that are commonplace in the primary classroom.

Identification

In light of the great burdens already placed on primary teachers, why add to this by introducing a need to identify able children within individual subjects? Identification of able children surely only makes sense when it is linked to effective provision and this, in turn, is linked to the individual child's rights. George (1997 p. 4) states that 'Educationalists are agreed that it is every child's right to go as far and as fast as possible along every dimension of the school curriculum in order to reach their considerable potential, and that this is one of the main aims of education'.

All children surely have a right not to be bored, but to be excited by their learning? Do gifted children merit special attention? Eyre (1997) notes that it was a commonly held belief that able children would always be successful, regardless of their circumstances, but that this has been disproved. Eyre states that research, such as that done by Freeman (1991), in her account of gifted children growing up, indicates that support and encouragement are vital to success. Eyre has summed this up in the model:

$$\text{Ability} + \text{Opportunity/Support} + \text{Motivation} = \text{Achievement}$$

Science is an ideal subject to provide motivation in the primary school because it is 'different' and it should be obviously different from any other subject. The provision of suitable opportunities and support is the challenge facing the primary teacher. The aim of this chapter is to give practical examples and ideas to help facilitate this within primary science lessons.

Methods of identification

The current trend towards increased emphasis on literacy and numeracy, often to the detriment of science, may well contribute to the difficulty of identifying a pupil who is able within this particular subject. What then are the characteristics of a primary aged pupil who is specifically able in science and are these different from those that would be exhibited in other subjects?

Of course some children are good all-rounders and are gifted in most subjects. However, we have personally met children in our teaching careers who are gifted in science but not necessarily in other areas. They have been articulate about their discoveries and have had an enthusiasm in science, which was far from evident in other subjects. One of these children was particularly memorable. He had a reputation as a 'naughty boy' whose behaviour often left much to be desired. He struggled with his English and mathematics and often ran out of patience. However, in science, if he was allowed to report his findings or express his understanding verbally, he could genuinely shine. His reply to the question at the end of the lesson, 'Who can tell me what they have learnt today?' was often staggering. This was obviously good for his self-esteem and it also showed a potential, which probably would not otherwise have been evident.

A child's lack of ability in literacy and numeracy may hinder their long-term progress in science, but this need not necessarily be the case at the primary level. As has been said, science is different and it is helpful to consider possible indicators of ability within this discipline. O'Brien (1998) emphasises the fact that the scientifically more able child does not just show good knowledge about science but that there are other characteristics that he says should also be evident, such as a vocabulary that is beyond other pupils of their age. The Dudley LEA (1998) note that the pupils who are highly able scientists are generally the ones who 'ask perceptive, provocative questions and bring background knowledge to their science'.

A checklist can be a useful tool for this identification process and can particularly help to maintain the subject specificity. The specific characteristics of able children in relation to science may include some or all of the following:

- a natural curiosity about the world and the way things work;
- an enjoyment of hypothesising;
- an ability to express scientific knowledge and understanding logically and coherently;
- scientific vocabulary used accurately and appropriately;
- an ability to transfer knowledge and understanding from one situation to another;
- an ability to spot and describe patterns in results;
- innovation in experimental design and/or in the collecting and recording of data.

Higher order thinking skills

As has already been suggested, science is a subject that is particularly suitable for extending children's thinking. In order to achieve this it is vital to depart from the feeling that often pervades – that science is an illusive quest for the 'right' answer – and to become aware that it is a huge and amazing subject. One of the great scientists, William Lawrence Bragg said: 'The important thing in science is not so much to obtain new facts as to discover new ways of thinking about them' (cited in Mackay 1977 p. 23).

Montgomery, in her evidence to the Education and Employment Committee (1999), suggested that teachers should change their teaching for able children from a 'competence based' to a 'cognitive based' curriculum:

> This would ensure children developed 'cognitive skills' such as thinking, planning, organisation, problem solving and creativity, and reflecting upon and monitoring their learning p. xliii).

Science lessons provide an ideal framework for this type of cognitive work and O'Brien (1998) notes that

> Children reveal something of their close understanding of science and the way they are viewing the world in the way they tackle thinking problems. It is therefore important for teachers to observe closely the way pupils think in science as well as what knowledge they display (p. 4).

O'Brien (1998), who is writing specifically with science in mind, goes on to state that the qualities that are desirable in children are:

- to be confident thinkers, clear about the means;
- the capacity to enjoy thinking and consider the beauty of the process rather than the chore of the operation;
- to consider concepts with care and not to dismiss them in haste;
- to trawl widely for ideas to encourage originality and creativity but to be on target with that breadth;
- to use the fine tools of thinking like a surgeon's knife for incisive conclusions.

This is an exiting list and sets out both the challenge and the potential for primary science.

The importance of thinking skills is acknowledged in the teacher's guide update to the Science Scheme of Work (DfEE/QCA 2000):

> By using thinking skills children can focus on knowing *how* as well as knowing *what* – on learning how to learn. Many aspects of science contribute to the development of thinking skills (p. 8).

The encouragement for the children to draw on their higher order thinking skills will be a feature that runs throughout this chapter and underpins most of the suggested activities or tasks. The inclusion of thinking skills in the focused learning objectives can add punch and challenge to the lesson.

Process and product

Montgomery (1996 p. 63) draws a valuable comparison between product based and process based curricula. She contends that 'content models emphasise the importance of learning skills within a predetermined domain', and that 'in these systems, a large amount of rote learning (learning material by heart) is seen'. The potential superficiality of such learning is highlighted. Process models cannot operate without a content base but the explicit teaching of investigatory and problem solving skills is predominant within this process model.

Our contention is that primary science for gifted and talented children benefits from a process based approach. At the heart of the process based approach is enrichment and extension of the curriculum, where the 'syllabus can be addressed in greater depth for the highly able' (Education and Employment Committee 1999 p. liv).

Constructivism

Constructivism is a commonly used model for science teaching in primary schools. This involves the elicitation of the children's current understanding of a situation and therefore also of their misconceptions. It works on the sensible premise that children do not come to lessons as 'empty vessels' but that they have already constructed their own ideas as to how the world works. This is equally true for able children. Harlen (1996) describes how the constructivist approach uses the children's ideas in a central role. These ideas then need to be restructured and this may involve: clarification and exchange, exposure to conflict situations, construction and evaluation of new ideas.

Constructivism opens up some interesting possibilities for extending the work with able children. The elicitation of the children's existing knowledge can be done in various ways, such as the use of concept mapping (Harlen 1996). Naylor and Keogh (2000) have developed a book of concept cartoons, which has many interesting possibilities. Each cartoon consists of a scenario, such as ice in a container, and a number of different explanations or questions posed by different cartoon characters. In the case of the ice the characters are offering different suggestions as to what happens to the weight of ice when it melts. The cartoons can be used to raise questions, elicit understanding and then as a springboard to take the children's learning forward. This could be through the development of practical investigations to test their ideas or through research.

Task setting

The setting of effective classroom tasks is a key area for consideration and there are some generally useful methods for challenging able children in science, such as:

- investigations;
- problem solving;
- the pupils acting as researchers;
- judicious use of questioning by the teacher;
- the encouragement of metacognition;
- the introduction of cognitive conflict;

- creativity;
- introduction to the 'big ideas' in science.

Each of these methods will be considered in turn.

Investigations

Investigations form one of the four main areas of science set out in the National Curriculum and so will be considered in detail later in this chapter.

Problem solving

'Problem solving is an effective way of challenging able children. Their interest is often gained by posing a question that is intriguing, and sustained by the motivation to puzzle something out,' Clark and Callow (1998 p. 32).

Problem solving involves the setting of activities, which require the pupils to draw on their scientific knowledge and skills to explore more complex ideas. The National Curriculum sets out the following skills necessary for solving problems:

- identifying and understanding a problem,
- planning ways to solve a problem,
- monitoring progress in tackling a problem,
- reviewing solutions to problems.

(DfEE/QCA 1999 p. 21)

The problems can be related to real-life situations, such as designing an alarm system, as will be described later. Problem solving can begin simply with a sequence of activities where children are getting first hand experience by 'playing' with science resources. This will allow children time to make free observations and work out ideas, which might then be developed into a solution to a problem. Key Stage 2 children might combine science and design and technology ideas to produce a lighthouse with a flashing light after exploring (playing with) simple circuits and switches.

Children as researchers

Porter (1999) highlights the need for gifted learners to be challenged through open-ended activities which include the opportunities for children to pursue their own interests to a depth that satisfies them. Allowing the children to act as researchers provides obvious potential for this to be the case. This research often needs careful direction from the teacher so that it is really challenging and motivating. This can be achieved in imaginative and interesting ways so that it goes beyond a simple request to find more about a particular subject.

Teachers' questions

Kerry and Kerry (2000) consider the centrality of teaching skills in improving able pupil education. They pinpoint effective questioning to be one of the key skill areas for teaching and point out that questions can be formulated to attract mainly lower order thinking or mainly higher order thinking:

Revision questions and those requiring only the representation of known material (simple comprehension) attract low order answers; while questions that ask students to deduce, hypothesise, analyse, apply, synthesise, evaluate, compare, contrast or imagine attract higher order responses.

(Kerry and Kerry 2000 p. 17)

It can also be advantageous to allow children to have time to consider questions, and Fisher (1990) suggests that giving children time to think, rather than rushing them to respond, encourages access to the higher order thinking skills. It can be effective to 'drop in' probing questions to a group of children and then come back later to find out how their thoughts and work have progressed.

Metacognition

Metacognition is the ability to reflect on our own thinking processes and, as has already been said, science is all about thinking so there should be ample opportunities for this within primary science. Children need to be encouraged to think deeply and also to be aware of their own thought processes. It has to be acknowledged that this can feel self-indulgent in the crowded curriculum, but it need not take a great deal of time and examples are given within the curriculum areas. Some teachers have introduced Bloom's Taxonomy to their pupils and encouraged them to consider which thought process they have accessed during the lesson. While this is probably only suitable for the oldest children in primary schools, it has interesting possibilities.

Cognitive conflict

Cognitive conflict occurs when a person realises that their accepted understanding of a situation is directly challenged, does not hold true and so needs to be adapted. Wood (1991) describes this as a state of conflict between what a child expects as a result of his or her interactions with the world and what actually transpires. In many ways, this process lies at the very heart of scientific thought, as the laws of science are constantly tested and reassessed. These laws are, in fact, merely sophisticated descriptions of the way in which nature works. Hence Newton's Laws of Motion hold true up to certain limits, but beyond these limits Einstein's Theories of Relativity take over. Even Einstein's theories are constantly under scrutiny and one of the joys of science is that it is a constantly developing subject.

Cognitive conflict can be used to challenge and then take forward children's thinking in a variety of ways. Asking children to hypothesise about the outcome of an investigation can introduce such conflict if the outcome is unexpected. The concept cartoons of Naylor and Keogh (2000), which have been mentioned previously, can also be used to encourage this process of cognitive conflict.

This possibility of generating cognitive conflict means that potentially the concept cartoons can be useful even with learners who already appear to understand the science involved in the situation . . . Older, more able and/or more knowledgeable learners can consider a wider range of factors which may be relevant to the situation and probe more deeply into underlying explanations (p. 7).

Creativity

Porter (1999) suggests the promotion and encouragement of intellectual risk taking – that is creativity – and divergent thinking for able children. Risk taking needs an atmosphere of acceptance so that children can voice their ideas and thoughts. Creativity can also be brought into science by recording work in imaginative ways, such as on posters, newssheets, taping or videoing. Children can act out the motion of atoms in solids, liquids and gases. Science theatres tour the country and often offer exciting insights into scientific knowledge. Again the concept cartoons can be a springboard to creativity as the children can be encouraged to make their own cartoons.

The big ideas

One of the inevitable, potential drawbacks of primary science is that the children can miss out on the excitement of some of the 'big ideas' of science. These are the theories that underpin the basic facts, such as the existence of atoms and electrons, or at the other end of the scale, galaxies and black holes etc. Richard Dunne, speaking at the Thinking Skills Conference (2000), highlighted the excitement of making connections between theories and examples. Able children can thoroughly enjoy this type of challenge. The big ideas often form a possible extension activity as they go beyond the primary curriculum. There is also a range of books, suitable for school libraries, that introduce these ideas in a fun way. Examples are given at the end of this chapter.

Examples of each of these methods have been considered under specific strands but are easily transferable to other areas of the science curriculum. References will also be made to the Science Scheme of Work (DfEE/QCA, 1998) because this is so often used in schools. What children are expected to know and understand is explained within each unit of this scheme. The statements also include an expectation for able scientists, which are useful when looking to extend this group of children.

The National Curriculum

Sc 1 Scientific Enquiry

As has already been said, science should be thought of as a mode of enquiry and not simply a body of knowledge to be learnt. In other words, it is about doing and not just knowing:

'Why', said the Dodo, 'the best way to explain it is to do it.'
Alice in Wonderland

This is exemplified in this area of the National Curriculum and it has exciting potential for extending able children, as investigations are inherently process based and have the potential to develop higher order thinking. Research by Coates and Eyre (1999) and Coates and Wilson (2000) indicate that highly able scientists at the end of Key Stage 1 are capable of working at Level 4 in Attainment Target 1: Scientific Enquiry. If we extrapolate from this, it seems reasonable to assume that Year 6 children who are able scientists should have the skills to deal with the concepts associated with Level 6.

Tables 4.1 and 4.2 below indicate how Attainment Target 1 of Curriculum 2000 can be directly linked to higher order thinking skills. In each case, these tables are followed by examples.

Table 4.1 Key Stage 1

Higher Level Thinking in Bloom's Taxonomy	Scientific enquiry: Sc1/AT1 Level 4
Application	• Where appropriate, children can make predictions.
Analysis	• In their own investigative work, they decide on an appropriate approach to answer a question.
Synthesis	• They begin to relate conclusions to patterns in data and to scientific knowledge and understanding. • They describe or show in the way they perform their task, how to vary one factor while keeping others the same.
Evaluation	• Children can suggest improvements in their work, giving reasons.

Example

In Unit 2E of the QCA schemes of work; 'Forces and movement', it suggests that some children (the most able) will 'explain how they made their comparisons fair and suggest several factors to investigate'. One of the teaching activities involves the children exploring cars rolling down ramps. Able children should eventually be expected to carry out a whole investigation, i.e. make predictions, design their own investigations, ensure fair testing, look for patterns in their data and evaluate the investigation to look for improvements. This would then mean using all of the higher thinking skills outlined in Table 4.1.

Table 4.2 Key Stage 2

Higher Level Thinking in Bloom's Taxonomy	Scientific enquiry: Sc1/AT1 Level 6
Application	• In their own investigative work, they (the children) use scientific knowledge and understanding to identify an appropriate approach.
Synthesis	• Children draw conclusions that are consistent with the evidence and use scientific knowledge and understanding to explain them.
Evaluation	• Children make reasoned suggestions about how their working methods could be improved.

Example

In Unit 6F 'How we see things', one activity involves children identifying factors which might affect the size and position of the shadow of an object. Able children would again be expected to carry out a whole investigation by suggesting questions that might be investigated, and then use their knowledge of light, shadows and the investigative process to devise their own fair test to try to answer one of the questions raised. They would be expected to make predictions based on their scientific knowledge before carrying out the investigation. Children should be expected to repeat measurements to check data and then present it in a line graph. Their conclusions would need to be based on the evidence of the patterns in their results (for example, the shape of the graph), related to their knowledge and understanding of light and compared with their predictions. This would allow them to evaluate the investigation in a systematic way, to examine both their original ideas and the method used in the investigation. Again this would involve the children using all of the higher thinking skills outlined in Table 4.2.

This ability to perform whole investigations needs careful teaching and a building up of skills and knowledge which will be discussed later.

Variables

We can develop the complexity, and hence the difficulty of an investigation, by changing the type of variables under investigation. There are three types of variables in an investigation which primary children will need to use. There is clear progression in their level of complexity:

1. Categoric – which is defined as descriptive or a classification. For example, the different types of magnet or the colour of a flower.
2. Discrete – which is defined as numerical, but taking only whole numbers or integers. For example, the number of layers of insulation around a can of water

or the number of seeds that germinate.
3. Continuous – which is defined numerically and can take any value. For example length, weight, volume, time and temperature.

We can illustrate this potential progression by examining an investigation involving parachutes. After a period of open exploration, play and discussion, children could be involved in the following investigations:

1. Which type of material makes the best parachute?
   Children could make parachute out of different textiles or paper and drop them at the same time to see which stayed in the air the longest. Children could draw bar chart from their data.
2. How does increasing the number of paper clips hanging from the parachute, affect the time of descent?
   Children would use one parachute and therefore need to time its descent to the floor with different numbers of paper clips attached. Children could again draw a bar chart from their data.
3. How does the area of the parachute affect the time of descent?
   Children would make parachutes with the same shape but different areas. They would then time their descent to the floor. Children could draw line graphs from their data.

Key Stage 1 children could be involved in each of the above investigations, but able children should be involved in investigations that involve discrete or continuous variables on some occasions, as in points 2 and 3. This might involve guidance from the teachers to steer children in that direction. However, we would not expect them to draw line graphs at Key Stage 1. Key Stage 2 children should also be guided to use continuous variables and then should display their data in line graphs. This will allow them to describe patterns in their data and link this to their scientific knowledge and understanding.

Degrees of openness

A second method of developing investigations and using them to differentiate, is the degree of openness exhibited by the task. There are three features of a science investigation that can be viewed in terms of how closed or open they are. This is illustrated in Table 4.3 (Jones, Simon, Black, Fairbrother and Watson 1992):

Table 4.3

Defining the problem	
Closely defined variables specified	➤ Not defined, variable not specified
Choosing a method	
Teacher tells pupils what to do	➤ Free choice of method
Arriving at solutions	
One acceptable solution	➤ Many acceptable solutions

The following examples of investigations illustrate the ideas.

a) Make cylindrical, cuboid and prism shaped pillars from the same sized pieces of card. Investigate which shape is the strongest by placing weights on them until they can hold no more.
b) Find out which shape of pillar will hold the greatest weight.
c) Investigate the factors that affect the strength of pillars.

Investigation (a) is closed in all areas. The variables are defined, the children are told what to do and one solution is expected: the cylindrical pillar will be the strongest. Investigation (b) is more open than investigation (a). The variables are defined, but the children need to decide which shapes to investigate and how they will carry out the investigation.

Investigation (c) has no variables which are specified and this task is therefore the most open of the three. The more open the investigation is, the more decisions the child needs to make and these are clearly related to the higher order thinking skills outlined in Tables 4.1 and 4.2. Able children at the end of KS1 should be involved in investigations in which at least one area is open, similar to Investigation (b). This investigation will involve the children in the skills of analysis and synthesis if they are to decide on an appropriate method and perform a fair test, and give them access to Level 4 in Attainment Target 1. At Key Stage 2 the able children should sometimes be involved in investigating where all three aspects are open. Again this will involve the higher thinking skills of analysis and synthesis and access to Level 6.

Concentrating on one area/skill at a time
Goldsworthy and Feasey (1997) note that it is very important for children to have opportunities to combine all of their skills together in a complete investigation, but point out that it is important to consider each of these skills in turn through direct experience and teaching. This is particularly true for younger children, as it can become a tedious chore for them to plan, obtain and present evidence, and consider evidence whenever they are involved in an investigation. Able children are the same as others in this context. It is important therefore, sometimes, to support or scaffold able children through the various stages of an investigation. Teaching can be planned to focus on one part of a strand of Sc1, for example, making predictions. Children need to be taught that a prediction in science should include a valid scientific reason which takes it beyond a guess. This involves children in applying their knowledge to a new situation. When presented with an investigation such as 'Can people with the strongest legs jump the furthest?' children will often state that people with the strongest legs can jump the furthest. When pressed to produce a scientific reason for this their argument often becomes circular, i.e. people with the strongest legs jump the furthest because they have the strongest legs. This requires the judicious and sometimes persistent use of questions to draw out children's ideas to form a reasonable prediction. The reiteration of the question 'Why?' may produce answers such as 'They need stronger legs to overcome gravity'. This

questioning process may take some time and it would then be appropriate for the teacher to support children more directly to plan and carry out the investigation.

This approach could be applied to many sections of Sc1 at Key Stages 1 and 2. The QCA Report, 'Standards at Key Stage 2, English, mathematics and science' (2000) noted that, since 1995, children generally succeeded on questions in the SAT papers which required them to read data from bar charts, graphs or tables. However, children were less successful on items that required interpretation of that data. As can be seen in Table 4.1 and 4.2 children need to user the higher order thinking skill of synthesis to achieve this. Interpreting data is one of the skills that able children have the potential to use, but direct teaching and practice of this is necessary for its development. There are a number of ways to achieve this. This might include examining data from other children in the class or from other secondary sources. Goldsworthy, Watson and Wood-Robinson (1999) have developed software and photocopiable resources which encourage the development of the skills needed for drawing and interpreting graphs. This is aimed at Key Stages 2 and 3 and so is appropriate for able children in the primary school. As this material is available for use on a computer, able children can work through this at their own pace.

Goldsworthy, Watson and Wood-Robinson (2000a) have concentrated on this development in another publication and again have included computer software. This considers in turn the different elements involved in an investigation. Among other things, they encourage pupils to consider, criticise and evaluate ideas or results gained by a fictitious group of children. As with their previous publication, described above, this is aimed at Key Stages 2 and 3 and may be particularly suitable for able primary children.

Sc 2, Sc 3 and Sc 4

Scientific enquiry, Sc1, should pervade the whole of the content of the National Curriculum for science and it is therefore impossible in reality to consider Sc 2 to 4 in isolation. However, for ease of reference, these strands have been considered individually and possibilities for the inclusion of scientific enquiry have been considered within each section.

Sc 2: Life processes and living things

Humans and other animals: research

Using the internet can be highly motivating for children, to help them find more about the natural world. A section of the website, QUEST, (http://www.nhm.ac.uk/education/quest2/english/whyquest.html) from the Natural History Museum of London, is particularly useful for extending able children within the context of Sc 2, life processes and living things. QUEST stands for Questioning, Understanding, and Exploring Simulated Things. It provides images of objects, such as a pollen grain or a skull, and allows children to make virtual observations, such as the weight and size, and allows them to view the object from all sides. There is a section that enables children to ask scientists for advice on better questions and a notebook to record and share observations. This website will help children to develop many of the scientific skills associated with investigations and encourage the use of higher level thinking skills.

The CD-Rom, The Ultimate Human Body (Dorling Kindersley 1994), is another example of extending children to allow them to investigate topics at a greater depth. The children could investigate how the heart and circulatory systems work and link this to their investigations. They could then feed back this information to the rest of the class. They would be using evaluation skills to firstly set out criteria for the information they are wanting to present, and then judging what information is relevant and why.

All primary age children have an interest in themselves and this is clearly reflected in the QCA schemes of work. Unit 5A, Keeping healthy, follows unit 2A, Health and growth, and Unit 1A, Ourselves, and all focus on this aspect of science. These units can contribute to the development of thinking skills in a number of ways. In each the children can develop their information-processing skills. For example, they could be involved in identifying, sorting, classifying, comparing and contrasting foods to identify the components of a healthy diet. Reasoning skills could be developed through Unit 5A where one activity asks children to 'speculate about factors which could change the pulse rate'. Children are expected to give reasons for their opinions, which are deduced from experimental data and other evidence available, and finally to explain how they have developed their ideas.

Investigations

At Key Stage 1 the children might investigate the pulse rates of different members of the class, and follow this up with an extension activity that examines the effect of exercise on pulse rate. This would involve the children in manipulating the continuous variables, for example the timing of the exercise, and making decisions about the method they would use to obtain data. This could be developed at Key Stage 2, where children might examine the connection between pulse rate and breathing rate. They would have to devise a test to compare pulse and breathing rates of people in different situations. The data could be then entered into a spreadsheet and plotted in a scattergram to check if there was a connection. This investigation would involve the children in manipulating more than one variable and again making decisions about the method that they might use to obtain data.

Physical fitness, and the aspects of life associated with this, comprise a second area that could be developed within these units. Key Stage 1 children might investigate the relationship between the size of their legs and the distance they can jump. Here the children would need to define the variable 'size' before they can undertake the investigation. It could be the length or circumference of the leg, for example. Devising tests to assess physical fitness and trying them out on a group in the class could form the basis of the investigative work at Key Stage 2. This investigation is completely open. The children will need to define what they understand by the term 'fit', decide which variables to control, which to change and which to measure and hence devise their own investigations. Alternative solutions to the investigation will arise, as different groups of children will be working on alternative ideas about fitness. This could be followed up with comparisons made between the experimental data and people's own perceptions of their own fitness.

The SATIS unit 'Getting to grips with training shoes' (Association for Science Education 1992) could also be used to extend this work. Parts C and D are applicable in this context as they examine the advertising of training shoes and 'Who buys them, and why?'. This will involve the children in active learning experiences where they are making decisions based on a relevant context. They are required to carry out a survey to determine what criteria children use when buying trainers and use this information to examine the aesthetic and scientific considerations in the minds of the consumers.

Green plants: Investigations

Examining the optimum conditions for plant growth and seed germination are science investigations which are very popular in school. Investigation might focus on whether plants need light and warmth to grow or the amount of water needed for healthy growth. The majority of children in the class might have very closed investigations where the teacher defines the problem and method for the children, for example, comparing two sets of seedlings, one set in a dark cupboard and another set in the light while keeping all other variables constant. Able children might simply be asked to investigate whether light and temperature effect plant growth. This will mean them having to devise their own method for the investigation. The same principle could be used in the QCA unit 3A, Helping plants grow well. The investigation involves children giving seedlings different amounts of water and could be adapted to be more open for the able children in the class.

Living things in their environment: Investigations

Strand 5 of Sc 2 requires children to investigate living things in their environment. The new unit from the QCA scheme of work, 5/6H, Enquiry in environmental and technological contexts, gives opportunities for extending children and developing their evaluation skills. They are expected to carry out research into factors affecting dandelions' growth in two different locations. The expectations for able children state that they will 'plan what to do and how to use available resources effectively; suggest limitations of the data collected . . . and how these could be reduced'. They will be making value judgements about their data and developing confidence in these judgements.

The Natural History Museum, London organises opportunities for children to take part in nationwide scientific study through the internet. The 2000 investigation was called 'Walking with woodlice' and set out to build up a UK data base after children had investigated their local environment and sent in their data. http://www.nhm.ac.uk/woodlice/page006.html

The children could investigate an environment, which is completely different from their own, for example, the rainforests:
http://passporttoknowledge.com has a link called 'Live from the rainforest'.
http://www.bbc.co.uk/education/landmarks is a website that examines the changes human population increases have had on five different environments.
This could give the children the opportunity to develop an in depth study and to use information in a selective way.

Sc 3: Materials and their properties

Grouping and classifying materials – metacognition and questioning

At Key Stage 2, pupils are expected 'to recognise differences between solids, liquids and gases, in terms of ease of flow and maintenance of shape and volume'. This is an area of the curriculum that is particularly suited to the encouragement of metacognition. It is probably easiest to begin by considering just solids and liquids. Our brains are wonderful things and we do not find it difficult to recognise a liquid when we see one or a solid when we bump into one! However, it is much, much more difficult to define, or put into words, what is meant by a solid or a liquid. It is a real challenge to accurately define the recognition process, which our brain performs almost instantly. This can be the source of a most fascinating discussion with children – or adults for that matter.

This can take the form of a whole-class discussion, begun by showing the children a selection of materials and asking them whether they are solids or liquids. This should include a wide variety of materials with varying properties. Children find it easy to spot water, vinegar, oil etc. as liquids, and bricks, sponges, chalk etc. as solids. The fun begins when they are asked to describe the properties of a liquid and how they are different from that of a solid. They will often describe a liquid as wet but what exactly does wet mean? They will tend to say that you can 'put your hand through a liquid' but then I can put my hand through sand in a sandpit! They will describe a solid as hard and can then be shown a sponge and asked if that is then a liquid.

In scientific terms, the definitions can be made short and sharp:

- a solid has a fixed volume and a fixed shape;
- a liquid has a fixed volume and no fixed shape;
- a gas has no fixed volume or shape.

Key Stage 2 children tend to be able to arrive, with pertinent questioning and prompting from the teacher, at the concept of a solid having a fixed shape while a liquid will take the shape of its container. This may well lead them to point out that sand or flour will take the shape of its container. However, of course, one grain of sand will have a fixed shape. Upper Key Stage 2 children may also be able to incorporate the concept of a fixed volume.

From experience of this type of discussion, it can really stretch children's thought processes and also increase the sense of awe about the functioning of our brains.

Asking the class to describe the difference between a cat and a dog can extend this further. Here is another case where our brain provides instant recognition but to define how this is done is a great challenge. As a quiet, seated dog can easily be distinguished from a cat in a similar position, their distinct barks, meows or walks are excluded from this definition!

Primary children can struggle with the concept of a gas and often associate it solely with a source of heat for cooking. As it is not possible to bring any of the coloured gases such as chlorine into the primary school, this can prove rather problematic. It is obviously not possible to see air but it is possible to see its effects, such as feeling the pressure when a finger is placed over the end of a bicycle pump and the piston is pushed in. A perfume bottle can be opened at the front of the class and children experience the fact that the gas spreads out to fill the container, in this case the room. They may well have experienced this more unpleasantly with a stink bomb! It is then possible to enter into an extension of the previous discussion and consider the characteristics of solids, liquids and gases.

The big ideas

As has been said, the children may well notice that a heap of sand will take the shape of its container and, in this way, it behaves like a liquid. The ball pool that is common in children's soft play areas is another example of this. At least one mother (an author of this chapter) has had to be restrained from diving in to rescue their child who disappeared under the balls in a ball pool, because the appearance was so similar to drowning! This may lead on to a very big idea, which is called kinetic theory.

Over the years, there has been some debate as to whether primary children should be introduced to the idea of the existence of atoms. Years ago, science teachers in training were taught that, according to Piaget's theory of development, children are not ready for abstract concepts until they are about 13 years old. As atoms cannot be seen and are therefore an abstract concept, this should be reserved for secondary school. It seems such a shame to deprive bright young children of the opportunity to enjoy this big idea. This is obviously an extension activity as it goes beyond the Key Stage 2 curriculum.

Children can be introduced fairly simply to the idea of atoms by considering the process by which the ancient Greeks arrived at an understanding of their existence. This takes the form of a 'thought experiment'. The children can be asked to imagine a block of, for example, pure copper. If this is cut in half, there will be half a block of copper; if it is then cut in half again, a quarter will remain, then an eighth and so on and so on. Eventually, a point will be reached where the smallest piece remains that is still copper and this is the copper atom. This is obviously impossible practically and hence it is solely a thought experiment, an exercise in philosophy. However, children do tend to be able to follow this process.

Kinetic theory is about the behaviour of atoms (or molecules but we need not worry about the difference at this stage) and this can be acted out by groups of children. In solids the atoms are closely held together and they cannot exchange their neighbours, they have some energy but just enough to 'jiggle' a bit. When they are given more energy, they can break away from their neighbours and move around but they are still fairly close together – hence they can flow and pour. Given even more energy, they fly off in all directions and so spread out as a gas.

Separating mixtures of materials: problem solving

Once the children have been introduced to the basic concepts within this area of the National Curriculum, it is possible to extend their thought processes by problem solving. They can be presented with various scenarios, such as the problem that the head's sugar has been spilt into the sandpit and she wants it back for her cup of coffee! There may have been a mysterious piece of writing and the author needs to be found. The author (conveniently) used a water soluble felt tip pen – can this pen be identified by using chromatography?

Chromatography is just the name for the characteristic separation of the dyes in a pen, which is achieved by placing a dot of ink on filter paper and allowing the paper to absorb water.

Sc 4: Physical processes

Electricity: Key Stage 1

This is a practical topic which pupils find highly motivational. Electricity is best delivered in a discovery mode. If children are shown how to set up a circuit, it can become a rather dry and arid task but if they discover it for themselves, it is very exciting. It seems sensible, in this case, to group the children according to ability, so that they can work through the open-ended tasks at their own pace. It is possible to structure these tasks so that there is logical progression:

1. Given a battery, wires and a bulb in a holder, make the bulb light.
2. Make the bulb light outside the holder.
3. Design a circuit which will test out which materials allow electricity to flow through them. Take this tester around the classroom and try out as many materials as possible.
4. Make more than one bulb light from the one battery.
5. Try out the other components, such as motors and buzzers.
6. Construct a switch, something which can be pushed or moved so that the electricity is turned on or off.

It is to be expected that the able children will work through these challenges at a faster pace than the rest of the class, but there is no reason to slow them up deliberately. They can then be encouraged to think of applications of their new-found knowledge, such as wiring up the doll's house or making a morse code transmitter.

Key Stage 2

It is best to use a similar structure of investigative tasks for the acquisition of the necessary skills to that used in Key Stage 1. Again, if ability grouping is used, the pupils can work through the challenges at their own pace and, if they finish quickly, they can be gainfully occupied.

The following challenges build on from those of Key Stage 1:

1. Make a bulb light and draw your circuit for posterity.
2. Construct as many different types of switches as possible.
3. Find out what happens to the brightness of bulbs when more than one is added to a circuit.
4. Find out if the length of the wires in a circuit makes any difference to the brightness of a bulb.
5. Given various circuit diagrams, construct the relevant circuits.
6. Make circuit diagrams for someone else to set up and predict the brightness of the bulbs in that circuit. They will tell you if you are correct!

In order to complete task 1 the children will, hopefully, spend a long time producing an artistic representation of their circuit. It is then a good time to show them that it is possible draw the circuit in two seconds flat in a way which any other scientist in the world will understand. Thus they can be introduced to circuit diagrams.

It is not required for the pupils to be introduced to parallel circuits in Key Stage 2 but it is inevitable that they will come across them when this type of investigative approach is used. It is probably best to explain that this is a special type of circuit, which produces some unusual results, such as the brightness of two bulbs and a battery being identical the brightness of just one bulb and the same battery.

Problem solving Key Stages 1 and 2

Once the basic skills have been grasped at each Key Stage, it is then possible to introduce problem solving as a means of challenge. This is so open ended that it can be used with the whole class. Ideally, the problem is best related to a real-life situation and requires the pupils to draw on their existing scientific knowledge. A little imagination may be required here.

An alarm system needs to be developed so that the teacher's lunchtime snack cannot be moved without a buzzer sounding or a light coming on. Perhaps the opening of the hamster's cage door will activate an alarm. Alternatively, it could involve a story, such as the king of a distant land who owns a priceless jewel, which he wants to display safely. The king could call for his scientific advisers (the pupils) to design a suitable system.

The big ideas

The idea of electrons (parts of atoms) flowing in the circuit could be introduced by the confident primary teacher.

Forces and motion: investigations

At Key Stage 1, children might investigate cars running down ramps, for example. All children should be allowed to play with the cars before deciding on questions that they might investigate. We would want able children to develop investigations that examined continuous variables, for example, what effect does increasing the height of the ramp have on the distance a car travels across the floor? This will give children access to Level 4 in Sc 1 and the higher order thinking associated with this. The play at the beginning of the activity is very important as it allows children to formulate their ideas in a concrete way rather than simply discussing what they might do.

Key Stage 2: questioning

The National Curriculum states that pupils need to understand that objects are pulled downwards because of the gravitational attraction between them and the Earth. It is very interesting to ask children why something falls to the ground. They are more than likely to say that it is because of gravity and think that this then explains all. The deeper question is 'But what is gravity and what causes it?'.

It is equally interesting to ask a selection of adults this same question. Very often this prompts such replies as:

'The magnetic core of the earth.'
'The spin of the earth.'
'The atmosphere pushing down on objects.'

In fact, none of these answers has anything to do with gravity at all. The gravitational force is a force that exists between all masses. Mass attracts mass! This does not seem at all logical because we do not feel a force of attraction when we walk past another person. At least, we cannot use this as an excuse to fall into their arms! It appears to be counter-intuitive. In fact, the reason we do not feel this force is because it is so small. I do feel the force of attraction between me and the very large mass of the earth.

I weigh less on the moon and so my muscles could make me jump considerably higher on the moon than on the earth. I would weigh less on the moon because the mass of the moon is so much smaller than that of the Earth. This leads to the interesting possibility of me winning the Olympics high jump – as long as I was competing on the moon and everyone else was on earth! Similarly, if you went to a planet which is much more massive than the earth, you would weigh more and you would find it very hard to jump and would feel very weighed down! Also if someone grew up on a planet which is much more massive than the earth, then presumably their muscles would adapt to this and be very strong, if they then moved to live on Earth they would be super strong (but no flying!).

Creativity

The idea of Olympic competitions on different planets has interesting possibilities for some creative writing.

Light: The big ideas

At Key Stage 1, children are expected to identify different sources of light and, at Key Stage 2, that light travels from a source. Light travels so quickly that this is actually a very hard concept to grasp. As Hollins and Whitby (1998) point out, when children first accept the presence of light it is 'just there' and is not understood that it travels. Many pupils have a 'person-centred' view of light, in other words we see because we look and light just helps. The concept of seeing because light travels into the eye requires some deep thinking.

The night sky can be used to develop this potentially big idea. Light travels faster than anything else we know but the objects in the night sky are very, very far away. Light from the sun takes eight and a half minutes to reach us. Light from the nearest star takes just over four years and light from other visible stars can take anything up to two million years to reach us. This means that when we look into the night sky, we see history. We see the stars as they were when the light left them.

Investigations

The programmes of study state that children need to understand about the formation of shadows. QCA unit 3F concentrates particularly on the formation of shadows when sunlight is being blocked. The introduction to the unit suggests that able children will understand that even transparent objects block some light. This can lead into a natural extension for able children to 'find out which sunglasses are the best'. This can take the form of a consumer test where children collect information about preferences on designs but more fundamentally to use light sensors connected to a computer to see how much light each pair of sunglasses will allow through. If a pair of eclipse glasses is included these let no light through but of course we cannot see through, them either. This unit requires children use information-processing skills. There is a suggestion that children should use secondary sources to investigate sundials. Able children could pursue this in depth and report back to the rest of the class.

Sound

We can extend a sound based topic by increasing the complexity of the work being studied. SATIS 3 Book 5 'Don't disturb dolphins' and SATIS 2 Book 6 'Bats' both examine echolocation. Children can study the habitats and environmental issues that have endangered these species. For example, the use of agricultural pesticides has reduced the number of bats. They can then go on to investigate reflection of sound, echoes, the way sound travels in air and water and humans' ability to echolocate. (More information about these can be found in the relevant SATIS books.) The bat work concludes with the children looking at ways to help these animals. This could be in the form of a letter to local newspapers or a poster and a leaflet, for example. The children could also give a talk to the rest of the class or the whole school. The dolphin unit culminates in the children taking on particular roles to give reasoned arguments about the environmental impact of setting up a small jet-ski operation in a seaside town. Both of these involve the children in using evaluation skills and making judgements about the issues raised.

Earth and beyond: questioning

Astronomy is, by definition, an infinite topic, which has huge potential for stretching the mind. The universe is awesome and wonderful. The content of the National Curriculum here is, of necessity, rather limited but its brevity should not hide the immensity of the topics it covers.

The pupils are expected to understand that the sun, earth and moon are approximately spherical. The fact that the earth is a sphere may seem blatantly obvious to the adult who has grown up with pictures of the Earth taken from space (and the ubiquitous school globe) but the theory was well established before the first space flight! In fact the idea of a spherical earth was established long before anyone sailed around the world. Yet the earth looks fairly flat to me! It is good to ask the children to consider the following question:

Before being able to view the earth from space by means of satellites, what was the evidence that the Earth is a sphere and is not flat?

This is an interesting discussion starter and it is surprisingly mind-stretching topic. Some of the evidence is as follows:

- When a ship disappears over the horizon, the last thing to be seen is the mast.
- The moon and the sun appear to be circular so perhaps the Earth is too.

This can be followed up with fairly obvious questions, such as 'Why do the Australians not fall off the earth?'. This is an area of the curriculum where it is essential to establish the pupils' existing understanding. This can be achieved by asking them to draw the earth, sun and moon as they would appear through the window of a space ship. The concept cartoons of Naylor and Keogh (2000) similarly can be used to elicit and challenge pupils' understanding.

The National Curriculum also requires the pupils to relate the spin of the earth to day and night and to understand that the earth orbits the sun once a year. Now this is a great deal of motion. We are inhabitants of an earth that is spinning on its own axis and revolving around the sun. This begs the question:
'Why do I not feel dizzy?!'

We are expected to believe that all this motion is going on and yet we feel nothing. Why not? This was, of course, one of the problems for poor Galileo when he put forward his idea that the earth rotates around the sun, rather than the accepted idea of the time that the sun rotates around the earth. It is equally interesting to ask adults the same question. Their responses are often similar to children's and a common reply is: 'We are moving so slowly that we cannot feel it.'

Now if the size of the earth is considered and the fact that it turns all the way around once every 24 hours, then it cannot be moving slowly – in fact, quite the reverse. The earth is also moving on a huge orbit around the sun once a year so it is, in fact, moving very fast indeed. The fact is that everything is moving with us and so we do not sense the motion. It is rather like being on a ship at night in a very calm sea – we would only sense the motion if the ship altered its speed.

Sis (1996), has set out Galileo's story in a picture book, which lends itself to use with Key Stage 2 children. It is a fascinating and poignant tale.

The scale of the universe: the big ideas

Hidden behind the earth and beyond curriculum then are some huge concepts and questions, but none more so than the awesome scale of the universe. These can be represented as rather bald facts as in Table 4.4:

Table 4.4

	Diameter (thousand km)	Distance from earth (thousand km)
Earth	13	—
Moon	3	400
Sun	1 400	150 000

However, it is almost impossible to grasp the meaning of these numbers and to get a feel for the scale involved. A useful demonstration is that of two small beads hanging by threads from a rod:

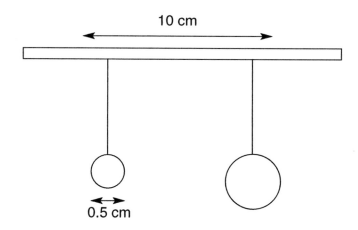

Figure 4.1

One bead represents the earth and the other the moon. One bead should be slightly larger than the other and they need to be about 10 cm apart. Children can then be shown a variety of possible models for the sun on the same scale: a golf ball, a tennis ball, a football and, finally, a large beach ball. They can then decide which would be about right for the relative size of the sun – the answer is the beach ball.

How far away does the beach ball sun need to be on this scale? It can be thrown to the middle of the class, to the back of the class etc. but this would not be far enough – it needs to be 40 m away!

It is also interesting to ask the children what is between the earth and the sun. Admittedly, there are two other planets between them but these are also relatively tiny and are in constant orbit around the sun. Children tend to have quite a crowded picture of space and think that there are other stars between the earth and the sun. Basically, there is just about nothing between us and the sun!

It is well worth asking the children where the next star to our sun would be. Incredibly, on this same scale with the sun 40 m away from the earth, the nearest star would be 4000 km away! So if the bead model is held up in a room in central England, the model sun is 40 metres away on the same scale, and the **nearest** star would need to be on the east coast of Canada.

Children as researchers

The earth and beyond is a natural topic for children to be given to research. There is a wealth of information available in textbooks, CD-Roms and on the internet. For example, pictures and information can be obtained from the Hubble telescope at:

http://www.stsci.edu/

By entering NASA into any of the search engines, a wealth of exciting sites can be found and up to the minute space news becomes available.

Resources

Books for children

Naylor and Keogh have produced a series of books which are based on the theme of their concept cartoons and are full of exciting questions designed to make children really think. They are a great way to stimulate children. Hodder Wayland publishes this series and the following titles are available:

The Seesaw and other science questions,
Upside Down Seeds and other science questions,
The Snowman's Coat and other science questions,
Bungee Jumpers and other science questions,
The Snowman's Coat and other science questions is also available as a Big Book.

Able children often have impressive memories and are sponge-like in soaking up information and they often love to grapple with big ideas. There are many science books that are written in an exciting and appealing way, such as:

What's the Big Idea series from Hodder Wayland:
Alien Life
Animal Rights
Artificial Intelligence

Chaos and Uncertainty
Environment
Food
Genetics
Nuclear Power
Time and the Universe

Science Museum Books of Amazing Facts series published by Hodder Wayland:
Communications
Constructions
Discoveries
Exploration
Inventions
Medicine
Space
Time

A lively and wacky *Science Magic* series from Oxford University Press:

Conjuring in the Kitchen
Brainwaves in the Bedroom
Laboratory in the Living Room
Bewitched in the Bathroom

Another lively and wacky series from Oxford University Press, this time:

How to clone a sheep
How to get to the moon
How to split the atom
How to build a time machine

Award Schemes:

The British Association for the advancement of science organises the BAYS First Investigators and Young Investigators schemes. Further details can be obtained by emailing: **elaine.stanley@britassoc.org.uk**

References

Association for Science Education (1992) *SATIS 8–14: Science and Technology in Society. Boxes 1–3*. Hatfield: Association for Science Education.
Bentley, D. and Watts, M. (1994) *Primary Science and Technology*. Buckingham: Open University Press.

Clark, C. and Callow, R. (1998) *Educating Able Children: Resource Issues and Processes for Teaching.* London: David Fulton Publishers.

Coates, D. and Eyre, D. (1999) 'Can encouraging the use of higher order thinking skills in science help young able children to achieve more highly?' paper prepared for the forth Summer Conference for Teacher Education in Primary Science, University of Durham, July.

Coates, D. and Wilson, H. (2000) 'Science Masterclasses for Able Children in Year 2'. In *SCIcentre 2000 and ASET Conference Report,* compiled by Frankie McKeon, SCIcentre, University of Leicester. Leicester: SCIcentre.

DfEE/QCA (1998) *Science. A Scheme of Work for Key Stages 1 and 2.* London: QCA.

DfEE/QCA (1999) *The National Curriculum. Handbook for primary teachers in England.* London: DfEE/QCA.

DfEE/QCA (2000) *Science. Teacher's Guide Update. A Scheme of Work for Key Stages 1 and 2.* London: QCA.

Diezmann, C. M. and Watters, J. J. (2000) Queensland University of Technology, Brisbane, Australia 'An enrichment policy and strategy for empowering young gifted children to become autonomous learners. In *Gifted and Talented International.* **XV** (1) Spring.

Dudley LEA (1998) *Meeting the Needs of the More Able Pupil.* Dudley: Dudley LEA Publication.

Education and Employment Committee (1999) *Highly Able Children.* London: HMSO.

Eyre, D. (1997) *Able Children in Ordinary Schools.* London: David Fulton Publishers.

Fisher, R. (1990) *Teaching Children to Think.* Cheltenham: Stanley Thornes.

Freeman, J. (1991) *Gifted Children Growing Up.* London: Cassell.

Gardner, H. (1994) 'The Creator's Pattern'. In Boden, M. A. (ed.) *Dimensions of Creativity.* Cambridge, MA: Massachusetts Institute of Technology.

George, D. (1997) *The Challenge of the Able Child.* London: David Fulton Publishers.

Goldworthy, A. and Feasey, R. (1997) *Making Sense of Primary Science Investigations.* Hatfield: Association for Science Education.

Goldsworthy, A. and Holmes, M. (1999) *Teach it! Do it! Let's get to it!* Hatfield: Association for Science Education.

Goldsworthy, A., Watson, J. R. and Wood-Robinson, V. (1999) *Investigations: Getting to Grips with Graphs.* Hatfield: Association for Science Education.

Goldsworthy, A., Watson, J. R. and Wood-Robinson, V. (2000a) *Investigations: Developing understanding.* Hatfield: Association for Science Education.

Goldsworthy, A., Watson, J. R. and Wood-Robinson, V. (2000b) *Investigations: Targeted Learning.* Hatfield: Association for Science Education.

Harlen, W. (1996) *The Teaching of Science in Primary Schools.* London: David Fulton Publishers.

Hollins and Whitby (1998) *Progression in Primary Science*. London: David Fulton Publishers.

Jones, A. T., Simon, S. A., Black, P. J., Fairbrother, R. W. and Watson, J. R. (1992) *Open Work in Science. Development of Investigations in Schools*. OPENS Project. King's College London: Association of Science Education.

Kerry, T. and Kerry, C. (2000) 'The centrality of teaching skills in improving able pupil education in educating able children', 4(2), Autumn.

Luxford, H. (1997) 'Where do I go from here? An approach to planning for enrichment in primary science', *Journal of NACE*, Spring Issue 1.

Mackay, A. L. (1977) *The Harvest of a Quiet Eye*. London: Institute of Physics.

Montgomery, D. (1996) *Educating the Able*. London and New York: Cassell.

Naylor, S. and Keogh, B. (2000) *Concept Cartoons in Science Education*. Sandback: Millgate House Publishers.

O'Brien, P. (1998) *Teaching Scientifically Able Pupils in the Primary School*. Oxford: NACE.

Porter, L. (1999) *Gifted Young Children. A Guide for Teachers and Parents*. Buckingham: Open University Press.

QCA (2000) *Standards at Key Stage 2. English, mathematics and science*. London: QCA.

Sis, P. (1996) *Starry Messenger*. Bath: Barefoot Books.

Wood, D. (1991) 'Aspects of Teaching and Learning'. In Light, P., Sheldon, S. and Woodhead, M. (eds) *Child Development in Social Context 2: Learning to Think*. London and New York: Open University Press.

CHAPTER 5

Information and Communication Technology

Chris Higgins

Introduction

Although Information and Communication Technology (ICT) is defined as a subject in the National Curriculum (DfEE/QCA 1999), in this chapter we shall not be considering the possibility of a child being gifted in the use of ICT (whatever that might mean) but rather we shall be interested in the uses that a child gifted in some other area may make of ICT to enhance their activity, thinking, learning and development in that area.

In one well-known discussion of forms of ability Gardner (1983), with his theory of multiple intelligences, proposes at least seven categories: linguistic, logical-mathematical, spatial, musical, interpersonal, intrapersonal and bodily-kinaesthetic. Using this categorisation, examples of ICT use can be found which could enhance activity in at least the first five of the domains.

ICT can be employed to do this in a variety of ways. It might be used to create an environment in which the child can practise and develop the higher order thinking skills of analysis, evaluation and synthesis as described in Bloom's taxonomy (1956), in the context of the given area. It could be used as a tool for exploring and enhancing a child's creativity. It might be the mechanism for promoting interpersonal relationships either by communication and interaction remotely at a distance or by creating an environment for collaborative activity face to face.

We begin our discussion by distinguishing between different ways of using ICT in the classroom and considering their merits. We shall then give examples of a variety of ICT applications and uses that can enhance thinking, learning and creativity for the gifted child, and finish with a discussion of teaching approaches that help to make use of ICT in developing what are termed powerful learning environments.

An important element of the ideas we shall be discussing is that the child needs easy, routine everyday access to computers. It should not be the case that they are available only in a separate computer room. That is an appropriate venue for teaching the basic skills, but there is an implicit message in always going somewhere special for ICT which says that it is not a natural part of the everyday classroom learning process. As Straker says:

> If computers are to be used as a resource to enhance and extend children's learning then they should be permanently available in all classrooms.

(Straker 1989)

ICT modes of use

One way to distinguish between ICT activities is to concentrate on the role that the computer plays in the activity. Three basic metaphors have been arrived at over time to describe the roles that the computer can play in the learning process: the computer as tutor, the computer as productivity tool and the computer as cognitive tool. We shall discuss these in turn.

The computer-as-tutor

This mode of operation covers the use of instructional software which has a long history, stretching back to B. F. Skinner's ideas in the 1930s of teaching machines and programmed learning. The idea of the computer as a child's personal tutor has long been popular in science fiction and the press. Although the reality is far removed from the image, there is some scope for the use of ICT in this mode with gifted pupils. The approach is based on the activity observed in the classroom known as the Initiation Response Evaluation sequence. Here the teacher asks a question or initiates a topic, provoking a response from the pupil. The teacher then passes judgement on the response either validating or invalidating it, and then usually initiates another topic. With the computer-as-tutor mode, the computer assumes the role of the teacher. For example, some pages of material can be presented on the screen and then a multiple choice question might be asked. The next step is determined by the child's response. Some more information may be presented, or confirmation of a correct response may be given, or some attempt might be made to diagnose the cause of an incorrect response. Feedback on correct and incorrect replies can be given, helping the child to identify errors and correct them. Many examples of simple instructional software on this model can be found.

The latest development in this area, and the one most often considered for use with gifted children, is that of sophisticated Integrated Learning Systems (ILS). These are an attempt to take the simple model towards the ultimate goal of the individualised curriculum. The approach is to provide a very rich, highly structured curriculum content and to attempt to customise each child's experience of it. There is no clear definition of the term ILS, but it is usually taken to mean extensive courseware linked to some management system (OTA 1988). This means that typically there will be three elements to the package: structured curriculum content with information, activities and tasks; a system for keeping records of the child's responses; and a management system which interprets the learner's response, determines their course through the content, identifies errors and determines actions to rectify them, updates the child's records and provides performance feedback to both the teacher and the learner.

The term Integrated Learning Systems is not actually appropriate, for what they really provide are instruction and indeed they are known as Intelligent Tutoring Systems (ITS) in the military and industrial training contexts where they originated in the USA. They lend themselves to training in discrete domains of knowledge where the material can be easily structured and are perhaps most successful in the primary context for areas of mathematics such as arithmetic and numeracy, where we can see a linear development of the content, and to a lesser extent in some areas of language, particularly grammar and spelling.

In their favour, ILS do address some of the needs of the gifted child. Most obviously, they allow them to work at their own pace and at their own level and, in situations where structured practice may be called for to assimilate certain skills or concepts, the ILS allows the child to practise their skills for whatever length of time is required to develop expert performance. Gagné (1982) discusses the idea of 'automaticity' where, for a learner to carry out a complex activity, some of the subordinate skills must be automatic. An everyday example can be found when driving a car: changing gear becomes an automatic process for an experienced driver but it required a conscious effort when learning. Gagné suggests that there are similar areas in reading, writing and mathematics where basic procedures need to be brought to a state of automaticity. For example, in mathematics, the basic algebraic skills of rearrangement of terms and so on when manipulating expressions are a prerequisite for both the effective solution of problems and the investigation of patterns.

Thus ILS can be seen as a means of managing both acceleration through a section of content, by allowing the gifted child to forge ahead on their own, and also enrichment of a content area by giving the gifted child the opportunity to explore content outside the regular curriculum.

There are, however, caveats to be expressed. Eyre (1997) discusses the disadvantages of effecting differentiation by work rate through a scheme of work. Some gifted children will view an ILS system with its structured curriculum as a motivating challenge, but others may view the prospect of a route march through seemingly endless stages with trepidation. Another possible drawback is that the activity is essentially solitary, and this may restrict the opportunities for constructive dialogue about the task in hand that might more naturally occur between the child and the teacher in other situations.

There is also a danger that the child's learning may be restricted by having to fit in with the software design, and they may find themselves driven along predetermined paths to solutions devised by algorithms with little opportunity for open-ended enquiry. Rodrigues (1997) reports a small scale study of a group of more able students working with ILS. Although the students were of secondary age, the evidence is illuminating. It was often found that the students could solve the problem presented to them but their answers, although perfectly plausible, were not accepted by the ILS so they had to work out how to match what was expected by the ILS algorithms. Although this might be said to be useful in making the children think in metacognitive terms about the activity, in practice the students felt it to be a fruitless exercise.

In general when using an ILS, instead of the child reflecting on their learning and constructing their own knowledge, the ILS provides algorithms which the child is required to understand and repeat in order to progress, and consequently the child will be concentrating on the lower order thinking skills of acquiring information and understanding content. As Papert (1980) warned 'one might say that the computer is being used to program the child'.

The Rodrigues study is one of a range of studies carried out in UK classrooms as part of a Department of Education commissioned evaluation of the benefits of ILS. Further details of the outcome of the evaluation can be found in Underwood and Brown (1997), which includes a comprehensive review of the current research in the area (MacFarlane 1997).

The computer-as-productivity tool

This is an obvious but nevertheless worthwhile mode of use. Following Kemmis, Atkin and Wright (1977) if we think of student activity as a form of labour then we can distinguish between 'authentic' labour – activities that are valued as they contribute to the intended educational purpose, and 'inauthentic' labour – activities that are essential for the task to be carried out, but which are not valued for their own sake.

The computer can be viewed as a productivity tool when it is being used as a means of reducing this inauthentic labour. This covers the use of such standard applications as word processors, desk top publishers, databases, spreadsheets, graphics packages, presentation mangers and so on when they are being used for specific tasks to support an activity. The computer can be thought of as a toolbox containing these discrete tools, and for the duration of the activity the computer becomes a single purpose machine such as a writing instrument or a data manipulation instrument.

For example, in a data-handling context the data can be swiftly searched, sorted and presented in a variety of graphical formats without the child having to spend time on the manipulation of the raw data or the preparation of the charts. Similarly, the use of a word processor, with its capability to amend and rearrange text effortlessly, means that the child does not have to waste time with laborious rewriting.

The computer-as-cognitive tool

This metaphor for computer use has its origins in the idea proposed by Vygotsky of psychological tools as instruments for the construction of higher mental functions. Pea (1985) introduced the term 'cognitive technologies' for these tools of the intellect such as written language, or systems of mathematical notation such as algebra: 'A cognitive technology is provided by any medium that helps transcend the limitations of the mind, such as memory, in activities of thinking, learning and problem solving' (Pea 1985 p. 168).

Salomon, Perkins and Globerson (1991) examine how the use of computer tools can enrich an individual's mind, and consider how a learner equipped with technology can achieve qualitatively better performance. They talk of an 'intellectual partnership' between the learner and the computer where the computer tool can take over some of the information processing that needs to be done, thus reducing the cognitive effort for the user. Spreadsheets, for example, can carry some of the load in terms of the calculations that the user could carry out themselves. Data-handling packages can present data in a variety of forms allowing the child to concentrate on the interpretation of the results. In a different vein, when working with simulations and models to investigate the variables in a system, the use of the computer allows the learner to shift their effort from memorising details of the system to hypothesising about the relationships within it.

Furthermore if, as discussed previously, automatisation of some low level operations is needed to enable higher order thinking to take place, then for a novice learner the computer can carry out some of the calculations, enabling the child to engage in higher order activities that they might not be capable of without the computer support. In Vygotskyian terms, working in partnership with the computer gives the learner the opportunity to operate in a zone of proximal development where the computer partner takes on the role of the more capable peer.

So we consider here those computer applications which can function as intellectual partners to amplify a child's thinking. They are the knowledge construction tools which help to facilitate higher order thinking.

ICT and the development of thinking skills

Having said that there may be a place for some use of the computer as a tutor for the gifted child, we shall now concentrate on the use of the computer as a cognitive tool and its role in the development and practice of higher order thinking skills, and problem solving skills.

If we consider how ICT is represented in the National Curriculum it is interesting that much of the discussion is couched in the language of thinking skills. Let us consider the three higher order elements of Bloom's taxonomy: synthesis – building a complex conceptual structure from simpler elements; analysis – breaking a conceptual structure down into its components; and evaluation – comparison of structures and making judgements about them. Eyre (1997) has a useful list of trigger words that help to identify classroom activities which involve these higher order skills. Using these it is striking to note how many of the requirements for ICT as set down in the programmes of study at both key stages (KS) are concerned with these skills in some form or another.

For example at KS1:

Developing ideas and making things happen
Pupils should be taught:

d. to try things out and explore what happens in real and imaginary situations.

Reviewing, modifying and evaluating work as it progresses
Pupils should be taught to:

a. review what they have done to help them develop their ideas;
b. describe the effects of their actions;
c. talk about what might change in future work.

and even more so at KS2:

Finding things out
Pupils should be taught:

b. how to prepare information for development using ICT, including selecting suitable sources, finding information, classifying it and checking it for accuracy;
c. to interpret information, check if it is relevant and reasonable and to think about what might happen if there were any errors or omissions.

Developing ideas and making things happen
Pupils should be taught:

a. how to develop and refine ideas . . .
b. how to create, test, improve and refine sequences of instructions . . .
c. to use simulations and explore models in order to answer 'What if . . .?' questions, to investigate and evaluate the effect of changing variables and to identify patterns and relationships.

Reviewing, modifying and evaluating work as it progresses
Pupils should be taught to:

a. review what they and others have done to help them develop their ideas;
b. describe and talk about the effectiveness of their work with ICT, comparing it with other methods and considering the effect it has on others;
c. talk about how they could improve future work.

(DfEE/QCA 1999, p. 98–101)

Furthermore, the National Curriculum draws attention to a number of Key Skills which are considered to be essential for effective learning, and one of those highlighted is information technology. Here again much of what is required is defined in the terms we have been considering:

The key skill of information technology includes the ability to use a range of information sources and ICT tools to find, *analyse, interpret, evaluate* and present information for a range of purposes. Skills include the *ability to make critical and informed judgments* about when and how to use ICT for maximum benefit in accessing information, in solving problems or for expressive work. The ability to use ICT information sources includes *enquiry and decision-making skills*, as well as *information-processing and creative thinking skills* and the *ability to review, modify and evaluate* work with ICT.

(DfEE/QCA 1999 p. 21 my italics)

The philosophy of working with ICT in the National Curriculum is that ICT should be carried out in context across the curriculum. Obviously there will be occasions where discrete ICT skills are worked on, but even then there will be a context in which the skill is practised. For instance, rather than talk about databases in the abstract, there will be occasions when data is collected, perhaps as part of a science activity. As one of the ways the children might work with this information, a database could be introduced and some of the facilities explained. They could then investigate the data to answer the questions they had started with, but also develop and practise their database skills in an authentic context.

Using ICT in context resonates with the idea of an infusion methodology for developing thinking skills whereby, rather than working on thinking skills in the abstract, contexts are identified within the curriculum where particular thinking skills can be developed naturally. We shall now consider a selection of ICT activities that encourage the development of thinking skills and problem solving skills in the various subject areas.

ICT activitities that develop thinking and problem solving skills

LOGO

LOGO is a programming language, the graphics capabilities of which allow the user to explore a geometric environment. One mode of use is to control a robot which moves on the floor. The child can control two movements of the robot, the distance it travels and the angle through which it rotates about its centre. These movements are echoed on the screen by an icon which draws a line as it moves, like an aeroplane leaving a vapour trail, so the child controls the length of the line drawn and its orientation. The original robots reminded the users of turtles as they scuttled about on the floor, so they were called floor turtles. By association the screen icons were called screen turtles and the whole activity christened Turtle Geometry. For older children the program is used without the floor turtle and they just work with the abstract geometric environment of the screen icon.

One of the main creators of the program, Seymour Papert, worked with Piaget and it was designed with Piagetian theory to the fore. The two modes of use were an explicit attempt to match two of Piaget's stages of intellectual development –

pre-operational thought and concrete operational thought. Papert's book *Mindstorms* (1980) discusses the philosophy behind the development of LOGO and his ideas for constructing self-contained computer environments with their own assumptions and constraints, or 'microworlds' as he terms them, for children to test their ideas and hypotheses about knowledge structures. LOGO is an attempt to create a microworld where the child could experience mathematics in a concrete form.

This is not the place to give a full description of LOGO, but we shall briefly mention those elements which are relevant to our discussion. For a fuller discussion of the use of Turtle Geometry see Abelson and diSessa (1981). In general the child manipulates the turtle with a combination of FORWARD and BACKWARD commands for movement and RIGHT and LEFT commands for turns, for example FORWARD 50 or RIGHT 90, effecting a movement forward of 50 units or a turn to the right of 90 degrees. The first powerful facility of the program is that a sequence of these commands can be defined as a 'procedure' with its own command name, and when this command is issued the sequence of basic commands is carried out. One of the commands in a procedure can itself be a procedure and this swiftly leads to the creation of complex conceptual structures from these few basic elements.

The next powerful element is that rather than issuing commands with specific numerical values attached, variables can be introduced which can be manipulated within the program. This can then be used in the other facility we shall mention, the ability to use procedures recursively. Recursion is the repeated application of a procedure, usually with the values of the variables involved being altered each time, and is carried out in LOGO by defining a procedure which refers to itself. The powerful combination of recursion and variables opens the way for many thought provoking mathematical investigations with which to extend the gifted child.

One of the benefits of ICT applications for mathematics are that they make concrete some abstract concepts. However, whereas in other types of program, such as dynamic geometry software, the effects are taken care of by the program, in Turtle Geometry the child has to engage with the mathematical nuts and bolts of the calculations to achieve their effects. As Piaget has it in one of his favourite aphorisms 'to understand is to invent', and by inventing LOGO procedures to create images the child is exploring their understanding of the geometric principles involved.

Beyond the important but purely mathematical context, we can also consider LOGO as the context for the development of general thinking skills and problem solving strategies. There has been an assumption that if children learn to programme computers this would have an effect on their higher order thinking skills. Much research has been carried out, particularly in America, and an extensive set of possible cognitive benefits has been suggested (see for example Feurzig *et al.* in Pea and Kurland 1987). LOGO lends itself particularly well to a number of them:

- the understanding of the need for rigour and clarity is useful in general problem solving situations, and the use of LOGO requires the development of rigorous thinking and precise expression in terms of the LOGO commands;
- the LOGO philosophy of debugging, whereby errors are seen merely as starting points for improvement, and attempts at a solution close in on the final answer, can be adopted as a standard approach to problem solving;
- the modular approach of breaking a problem down into smaller subproblems, which can be tackled separately, is inherent in the way LOGO procedures are assembled as building blocks for creating larger conceptual structures;
- an awareness of the metacognitive processes of problem solving and the choices to be made between solutions can be fostered by LOGO, as it provides the language for the explicit discussion of problem solving;
- working with LOGO develops a facility with a range of heuristic problem solving strategies. Polya (1945) and Schoenfeld (1985) have written extensively about such strategies in a mathematical context and Papert himself said that the LOGO approach exemplified Polya's ideas. For example: deciding on a plan of campaign for how to tackle a problem can be mirrored by the decisions taken when deciding on the order for procedures to be carried out; and comparing the current problem to similar ones to see if known solutions can provide an insight into the given problem, relates to the idea of modifying existing LOGO procedures when faced with similar tasks.

However, research has shown that although there is evidence of mathematical learning when LOGO has been used as a pure Piagetian discovery environment as first envisaged by Papert, there are no discernible effects in terms of the development of thinking skills (see for example Pea and Kurland 1987; Pea et al. 1987). All is not lost, though, and we shall see how this might be rectified when we consider later how we might provide powerful learning environments with ICT.

Hypermedia

Hypermedia provides a mechanism for the organisation and presentation of information. It derives from the idea of hypertext, a term first defined in 1967 to mean non-sequential arrangements of text, with pieces of text known as 'nodes' connected by 'links'. Although most text is presented linearly, the mind does not associate ideas this way and hypertext was an attempt to represent the non-sequential form of mental processes. In its ICT form the node text is displayed on the screen together with its associated links in the form of particular highlighted words or special icons. Pointing at the link with the mouse and clicking activates it, and the node text at the other end of the link is displayed, together with its links.

Hypermedia is the extension of this idea to include multimedia resources as nodes – text, images, sound, animations and video material. CD-Roms and Internet websites are examples of hypermedia. In some sense a presentation manager such as Powerpoint could be said to be a simple form of hypermedia, as it does allow the creation of screens (nodes) with text and images, but the linking structure is severely restricted as the screens are usually presented sequentially in a linear format. Full hypermedia authoring packages are now available for the classroom and we shall consider their possibilities.

Eyre (1997) suggests that one method of extending gifted children is to present the challenge of recording information in unusual ways. Marcus (1991) observes that hypermedia documents:

> provide extraordinary opportunities for students to show what they know – and feel. The expressive repertoire of students is enormously enriched by these high-tech resources, which add new and wonderful dimensions to the term 'language arts'.
>
> (Marcus 1991 p. 15)

Creation of a hypermedia document first requires the child to assemble the individual elements that it is to contain. These might be original text written by the child or imported from another source and edited. Images could be drawn in a graphics package or created in another medium and then scanned in. Photographs could be imported from a digital camera, audio elements could be recorded, video clips could be added and resources could be downloaded from the Internet. Choices have to be made about what to include and what to omit. This process requires evaluations to be made of the material and editorial decisions to be taken about what is important and relevant.

The information then has to be organised into the nodes and decisions taken about linking the nodes in meaningful ways. The child is going through the processes of constructing their own knowledge in an authentic context. They have become knowledge architects and are creating meaningful clusters of ideas with multiple linkages, much as experts in a knowledge domain do.

One of the powerful elements of the hypermedia packages is that the process can be managed via the 'storyboard', where miniature representations or 'thumbnails' of the screens can be viewed and then repositioned within the document by clicking and dragging on the storyboard. There is also a strong visual element to the process of structuring the information as the child can choose from a variety of visual metaphors to help them create their own cognitive structure for the knowledge. These metaphors are also useful as navigation aids for the eventual viewer of the document.

In an information-rich subject like science, the production of a hypermedia document can be used as a way for a child to draw together the outcomes of research and investigation into a given topic. A book metaphor could be employed to arrange the material in a hierarchical structure with the initial screen functioning as a contents page, with links to sections on the various items which then consist of pages to be turned. Another approach in a scientific context might be to work from an initial picture or diagram with links from parts of the picture to sections of description. An experiment could be reported which was structured in terms of an introduction, the progress of the experiment and a report of the results with elements of text, graphics, photography and even a voiceover.

Other metaphors suggest themselves for other subject areas. For example, suppose a local history investigation has been carried out researching the local village, its buildings and the people who have lived in them. One approach to organising the wealth of information collected would be to start with an initial node of a simple map of the village, to give a feel for the relative locations of points of interest. This could be an image scanned in or created with a graphics package. Links could then be made via icons representing particular buildings to nodes with pictures and text describing the history, architecture and construction of the buildings. From these nodes, links could return to the original map or other links could go to nodes with information about the occupants of the buildings. Another link from the original map could be to a timeline of events in the history of the village, each of which could be represented by an icon linking to nodes with further information and illustrations. Other links could be to maps of the village from previous eras to give a feeling for how it had developed over the years. The multiple representations of the information in ways relating to the physical organisation of the buildings or the chronology of the timeline are powerful aids for the children in making sense of the mass of information.

In a different vein, hypermedia can be exploited as a mechanism for exploring literacy. One approach in writing hypertext is to create a document essentially like a book, consisting of continuous prose with diversions like footnotes to support explanatory or extension material. A different approach is to work with the facilities of the medium and use it to create branching stories. The gifted child can then explore the possibilities of parallel storylines or multiple endings. Yet again the nodes could be structured like the scenes in a play and plot development and dialogue could be worked on.

A combination of both of these approaches takes us to something like an adventure game. Adventure games are essentially hypertexts, where the programme reacts to responses from the user by deciding which link they correspond to and activating it. Children can use hypermedia authoring to create their own adventure games by writing text segments and then offering their readers options as to how to proceed in terms of links to other text. There are two main activities in writing such stories: the first is structuring the text nodes and the second is writing the text that advances the story and includes both description and hints or puzzles within the text as to how to proceed.

A contrasting literary approach to these story-like structures is to use the hypertext as a commonplace book, somewhere to collect together extracts culled from other sources, a repository for information where items are collected together and links created to represent associations between the elements. Such a hypertext can form the research phase for a later piece of work, providing the raw material which can be worked on to produce a linear text, or it can stay as a piece of work in its own right, being extended and elaborated over time.

Concept mapping software

Concept maps are intended to represent the knowledge structures that people have in their minds. They are based on a cognitive model which considers that human memory is organised semantically, that is according to meaningful relationships between ideas. The ideas are arranged in what are called 'semantic networks' of interrelated concepts. Concept maps are visible representations of these semantic networks, consisting of graphs with nodes representing concepts and labelled lines representing the relationships between them.

The psychology of learning distinguishes between declarative learning (knowing about something) and procedural knowledge (knowing how to use that information). Semantic networks represent structural knowledge, showing the 'knowing why' links between 'knowing what' and 'knowing how' (for more discussion of the background to semantic networks see for example, Jonassen 2000).

As an example, Ghaye and Robinson (1989) describe five types of link relevant to geography, together with examples of words used by children to label each type (other concept domains might require different types of link):

Structural: expresses a taxonomic or hierarchical relationship between concepts;
Functional: expresses a function, purpose or use;
Locational: locates concepts in space;
Procedural: expresses an order, progression, precondition, process or prerequisite relationship between concepts;
Logical: expresses a logical or conditional relationship between concepts.
(Ghaye and Robinson 1989 p. 131)

These might produce a concept map such as Figure 5.1:

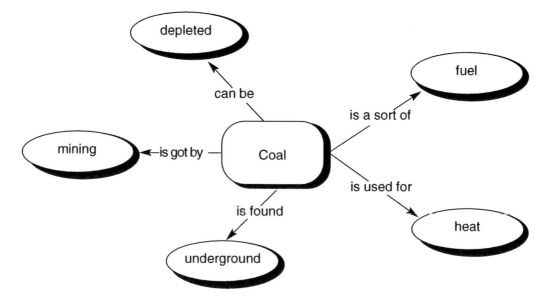

Figure 5.1 Concept map

In passing, we should note that the structure of a concept map with its nodes and links is reminiscent of that of a hypermedia document, and constructing a concept map can be used as part of the planning process when designing a hypermedia document.

One of the main benefits of getting the gifted child to create concept maps is that it requires them actively to reflect on their learning. The process allows them to make explicit what is often implicit and provides a vehicle for the discussion of their ideas and their relationships. Taking a constructivist approach, meaningful learning takes place when new ideas are related to the knowledge that the child already has and when they see how ideas are related to one another. Creating concept maps allows the child to externalise their current knowledge and helps them integrate the new concepts into their existing frameworks. They reconceptualise the knowledge domain by adding the new ideas and refining their understanding of what they already know.

Concept mapping software aids this process as it allows the child swiftly to add to, amend and manipulate the nodes and their connections. Clicking and dragging allows repositioning of the elements effortlessly and the programs have some inherent organisational facilities that can be adopted to aid clarity. In this way the software provides opportunities for easy visualisation and experimentation. To use concept mapping effectively requires some experience. Jonassen (2000) suggests a sequence of activities that can be followed, and a detailed discussion of strategies and activities for introducing the ideas of concept mapping to different ages of children can be found in Novak and Gowin (1984). In brief the following stages should be employed:

- establish the domain to be considered;
- identify the important concepts;
- define the nodes;
- construct the links;
- elaborate and expand the network;
- reflect on the process.

A spin off from the creation of a concept map is that it can be used as a diagnostic tool to help assess a child's understanding of a topic. You can carry out a qualitative analysis of the structure of the map and a quantitative analysis of the linkages (for further details see for example Jonassen, Reeves, Hong, Harvey and Peters 1997). However, the possible benefits of using them as assessment tools should not be allowed to conflict with the benefit to the child as a cognitive tool. Often the most meaningful learning will occur for the child when they are allowed free choice over the elements of their concept maps, but this will result in very idiosyncratic results, difficult to assess. Restricting the exercise to a given set of concepts and prescribing the link descriptors to be used will produce maps which are easy to assess, but this presupposes a correct version of the knowledge structure which goes against the constructivist intention of the activity.

Simulations

Simulations provide a model of a real or imaginary situation for the child to explore and investigate. The purpose of modelling a situation is to highlight implicitly the most important elements by including them in the model, making the situation easier to understand by removing some of the clutter and confusion of reality. The child interacts with the model by entering data, taking decisions, making choices or responding to questions and then observes the effects. In this way it is hoped that the child will discover relationships between the elements involved, construct their own knowledge model and develop an understanding of the key concepts as the underlying model is revealed.

Simulations can be used to explore imaginary scenarios peopled with fabulous characters, or realistic scenarios which in practice would be difficult for the children to explore. They encourage a playful approach to learning. They can give a meaningful context to tasks so that the child's activities are enhanced with a sense of purpose. The situations are repeatable so that the child can learn to explore them in a systematic way. If they are unable to solve a particular problem, or are unhappy with the outcome of a particular decision, they can repeat the program after having discovered a solution or reconsidered their actions, and retrace their steps to wherever they were in the program and then continue with their new course of action.

As well as providing opportunities for developing thinking and problem solving skills, simulations can also be environments where children can collaborate with each other and thus provide opportunities for the development of interpersonal skills. We shall return to that aspect in the next section, but for now we concentrate on the thinking and problem solving skills.

A fundamental element of real-life problem solving is the need to start by clearly defining the problem. Often in a classroom context there is an artificiality to problem solving in that the child is presented with a problem to solve out of context. In a simulation they must decide what the problems are, in the sense of what must be done next, and then must marshal the material and ideas to solve them. Employing the heuristic problem solving strategies mentioned previously, they might next consider if they have encountered a similar problem before and, if so, whether they can modify their previous solution. If faced with a situation with a number of interrelated variables they might develop a systematic approach to investigate the effects of each of them. Often the child will need to identify the known and unknown elements of the problem, deciding what information they have and what they still need to discover. Finally, they will need to employ reasoning, decision making and creative thinking to carry out their plans.

Throughout they will need to employ a battery of general problem solving techniques such as making notes, keeping logs, drawing up tables and sketching maps. At each stage they will need to reflect on where they are with the simulation, what they have discovered so far and then make a plan about how to proceed. All these activities require higher order thinking skills to be successful. At the end of the activity the children should be encouraged to step back and evaluate what they have been doing. As Montgomery (1996) says:

> Characteristic of all simulations is that they must be followed by a discussion-debriefing session to discuss what transpired so that educational and meta-cognitive objectives can be achieved.
>
> (Montgomery 1996 p. 17)

They might consider how authentic the simulation has been and assess its validity by comparing it with their experiences from other sources. They could also reflect on the differences between the simulation and reality where not all variables are so easily controlled or their effects so easily measured.

Further to the last point, as well as the simulations written for educational use, there are now large numbers of programs written for the home entertainment market which use the simulation format, and which could lend themselves to use in the classroom. They have the benefit of much improved graphics and game-play. Their complexity can, of course, be a problem in educational terms as, although it might be more realistic, it may be difficult for children to explore systematically if it is not easy to see the effects of any decisions that they take. However, with careful organisation and clear objectives a program such as Sim City, which requires the children to design and build a city which then develops over time, can be used successfully. One bonus with many of these commercial programs is that they include an option which allows the children to edit the scenarios in which the game takes place. For many children this activity can be as interesting and thought provoking as the simulation itself as they can investigate the rules driving the model. So, for example, in Sim City, the geographical location where the city is to be built can be created to represent a known location. This requires the children to get involved in a range of activities interpreting maps, making calculations and estimations, and transferring data into the program to recreate the topography of the actual site.

ICT and interpersonal skills

Contrary to the popular image ICT need not always be a solitary activity. Many classroom activities involving ICT can be the forum for collaborative work, providing opportunities for discussion and reflection with peers and for the development of interpersonal skills. Simulations in particular can be a productive arena for children's collaboration, but other activities can also perform the same function, such as a piece of collaborative writing with a word processor, or the use of a CD-Rom or the Internet for the research of a topic.

In fact, as well as providing for the development of interpersonal skills, Laurillard (1992) reported that the collaborative use of simulations was more effective than solitary use. She suggested that this was because, when working in pairs, learners spent more time discussing plans of how to proceed and reflecting on the outcomes of their actions than learners working on their own did. This engagement with planning and reflection meant that they developed an account of what was going on in the simulation, which was more capable of being generalised than was usual when a learner attempted the simulation on their own.

The benefits for children working together will depend to a large extent on how they interact. In the early 1990s the Spoken Language and New Technology (SLANT) project looked at a large number of primary school children working together at computers, but found that the educational quality of the talk was disappointing as discussion rarely developed (reported in Mercer 1995). The project came up with a definition of educationally desirable talk as follows:

> Exploratory talk is that in which partners engage critically but constructively with each other's ideas. Statements and suggestions are sought and offered for joint consideration. These may be challenged and counter-challenged, but challenges are justified and alternative hypotheses are offered. In exploratory talk, knowledge is made publicly accountable and reasoning is visible in the talk.
> (Mercer, Wegerif and Dawes 1999 p. 97)

From their research results and their theoretical analysis, the project members proposed the following set of ground rules for classroom discussion, which they felt could be taught to children and would help facilitate and generate this exploratory talk:

- all relevant information is shared;
- the group seeks to reach agreement;
- the group takes responsibility for decisions;
- reasons are expected;
- challenges are accepted;
- alternatives are discussed before a decision is taken;
- all in the group are encouraged to speak by other group members.
> (Mercer, Wegerif and Dawes 1999 p. 98)

There is some debate about what the general benefits would be to gifted children of working collaboratively (see Porter 1999), but in this context they can be summarised as the opportunity to practise oral communication, the need in discussion to explain their thinking more clearly and make their ideas explicit, and perhaps even the opportunity to teach their peers. It is a truism that the best way to learn something is to attempt to teach it to someone else, and as Montgomery (1996) says: 'Teaching is the one method which can ensure 90–100 per cent understanding on the part of the teacher'.

Another aspect of developing interpersonal skills can come from the use of the communications element of ICT. The gifted child often has interests beyond the scope of the ordinary school curriculum and resources, and a need to interact with others with similar interests and abilities. As for resources, CD-Roms and Internet websites can provide access to information and material far beyond what has been available by traditional means. The use of email can fulfil the need for interaction by putting them in touch with a community of like-minded individuals, either by email or through Internet discussion groups. A fine example of such a site is NRICH (http://www.nrich.maths.org.uk) produced by the Mathematics Enrichment Programme based at Cambridge University. This offers a variety of web-based resources to enrich the mathematics curriculum. There are problems to solve, games to play, articles, pupil and teacher discussion areas, teacher resources and opportunities for children to ask questions of practising mathematicians. It provides an environment to induct children into the culture of being a mathematician.

The Internet can also allow the gifted child access to experts in a particular field, as more and more the norm is for such people to have a presence on the Internet via personal websites. Using email teaches the child the skills of interacting at a distance through this new medium, which is a hybrid halfway between speech and text, more akin to sending an electronic postcard. These same mechanisms can also help to address a problem raised by Freeman:

> They need help with their special vocational problems, because the many talents that some possess cause difficulties for them in choosing how best to direct their lives. They can be supported through regular communication and interaction with others of like mind.
>
> (Freeman 1997 p. 55)

The latest development in this field is the creation of virtual reality environments where the child can create an avatar, a computer representation of themselves, which they then guide in real time through the environment to interact with other children's avatars. The communication element is essentially little more than synchronised email but the thought that could go into the design of the avatar and the possibilities for role play could be fruitful.

ICT and creativity

Kozma (1991), in reviewing the research on learning with different media to investigate whether their different characteristics influenced the structure of learners' mental representations and cognitive processes, found that it was the transformational capabilities of ICT that are crucial. The provisional nature of ICT material, which allows changes to be made easily, encourages the exploration of alternatives. The interactivity of ICT, characterised by rapid response and dynamic feedback, fosters evaluation and judgement of the product even as it is being created. The effects of these benefits can be seen in many situations. The writing process for a gifted child can be more like that of a professional writer with drafting and redrafting stages which would be difficult to ask for if everything was handwritten. Some gifted children have difficulty expressing themselves in the written form, and it may be that ICT, with the advent of more powerful voice input software for word processors, will become a valuable tool for them.

Dynamic geometry packages allow children to explore a geometric environment by interactive construction, and investigate such concepts as symmetry and transformation by manipulating points on screen. The geometric construction redraws as the image moves thus giving a sense of concrete reality to an essentially abstract phenomenon.

The most obvious area for creativity is perhaps art, with the proliferation of graphics packages. Not only art as a subject but also the elements of art and design in terms both of creating images and of the aesthetics and effectiveness of image and layout, that naturally arise when creating hypermedia screens or carrying out desk top publishing. ICT provides the possibilities for working with images which are similar to those of two other traditions – painting and photography. Art packages mimic traditional painting processes for creating images, and the photographic-like element of ICT allows children to capture images in a variety of ways and then manipulate them.

In any artistic medium there are a variety of techniques and processes which can be employed. The artist develops the craft skills for interacting with the medium and in the process develops an understanding of the potential and the constraints of the medium. When considering the creation of images with a graphics package there are two possible types of activity. First, there are those that mimic a painter, such as use of a brush, colour wash and so on, and second, there are those that enhance the image by transformation effects. The child uses a tool, say a brush, pen or spray can, for a particular effect and draws by clicking and dragging with the mouse. As well as drawing freehand, there are tools for drawing with mathematical precision that give accurate representation of straight lines, rectangles, polygons, circles and ovals. One power of the ICT medium is that the user can undo the last action without damaging the picture, so children can experiment with colours and textures more readily than with traditional painting. Another is that the child can copy parts of the image and experiment with the transformational aspects of the package. Learning the craft skills are part of the computer as a tool scenario, but it is with the transformational capabilities that the child enters into the computer as cognitive tool area.

ICT and powerful learning environments

Using ICT, as we have discussed, to develop thinking skills and creativity requires some specific teaching approaches. De Corte (1990a, 1990b) identifies powerful learning environments as those that promote higher order thinking and transfer of learning to other contexts, and considers that they are: 'characterised by a good balance between discovery learning and exploration on the one hand, and systematic instruction and guidance on the other. (De Corte 1990a p. 74).

ICT can play a major role in creating such environments. Freeman (1997) suggests that one of the aims of working with gifted children is to help them become autonomous learners, but on the other hand research shows (Coates *et al.* 2001) that we must not lose sight of the fact that gifted children need to be taught some of the time as well – skills, concepts, strategies and so on. The cognitive apprenticeship model of teaching (Collins, Brown and Newman 1989) addresses both of these aims and sits well with our attempts to create a computer supported powerful learning environment.

The model is based on the ideas of situated cognition, which argues that knowledge is constructed as a product of the activity, context and culture in which it is developed and used, so teaching something abstracted from the situation in which it is learnt and used limits the possibilities of learning. This matches our philosophy of using ICT in context and developing an infusion methodology for the development of thinking skills.

Collins, Brown and Newman (1989) suggest that to explore the ideas of concepts being situated and developed through activity we should consider conceptual knowledge as similar to a set of tools. This echoes our references to the mental processes involved in thinking as skills, and leads us to consider how one traditionally learns a skill or how to use a tool. Learning how to use a tool effectively requires more than a list of instructions. It also requires an understanding of the purposes it can be used for and the ways in which expert practitioners use it. So learning is most effective when it takes place in authentic situations with experienced practitioners to guide and inform the learner. One of the reasons for ICT being an element in the construction of powerful learning environments is the possibilities it offers for provision of circumstances in which authentic activities can take place.

Collins *et al.* developed the cognitive apprenticeship model by adapting elements of the traditional craft apprenticeship to the sphere of education. They analysed a number of successful examples of teaching in the foundational domains of reading, writing and mathematics which adopted these approaches. Combining their analysis with the ideas of expert scaffolding most commonly associated with Wood and Bruner (Wood *et al.* 1976) they proposed the model of cognitive apprenticeship for the design of learning environments.

The model identifies four dimensions to a learning environment: the content taught, the pedagogical methods employed, the sequencing of learning activities and the social context for learning. We shall concentrate on the pedagogy, mentioning the other elements only briefly.

The consensus in cognitive psychology concerning content is that the categories of knowledge required by an expert practitioner can be summarised as: *domain specific knowledge*; *heuristic strategies* for tackling tasks and problems; *metacognitive control strategies* for managing the activity; and *learning strategies* enabling learners to develop the other three types.

The guiding principles suggested for sequencing of learning activities are not unexpected: practise *global skills before local skills*, so that the learner develops a feel for the whole task before concentrating on the details; develop *increasing complexity*, so that the learner only requires a small amount of domain knowledge at first; and develop *increasing diversity*.

As regards the social context for the learning, the model proposes that the following are characteristics of a social context that encourage motivation and a positive approach to learning tasks: *situated learning*, enabling students to see a purpose for their learning and be able to tell when it is appropriate to apply it; *community of practice*, consisting of opportunities for communication about different ways to accomplish tasks, encouraged by common projects and shared experiences; *intrinsic motivation*, which can be strengthened by encouraging the setting of personal goals rather than by relying on reactions to external requirements; and *cooperation*, encouraged by working together in groups, in pairs, in competition with other groups, or not, as the situation demands.

We now come to the pedagogy involved, which is the heart of the cognitive apprenticeship model. The model suggests the following ways to promote the development of expert performance:

- *Coaching* – the teacher observes the students carrying out the task while offering feedback and prompts to bring their performance closer to that of an expert.
- *Scaffolding* – the teacher provides support to the student while carrying out the task. This could take the form of suggestions, written materials, or actually carrying out part of the task for them. This idea obviously derives from the Vygotskyian concept of the zone of proximal development. An integral part of the process is the diagnosis of a student's current ability and the gradual removal of support or *Fading* until the student is on their own.
- *Articulation* – this includes any techniques for getting the student to make explicit their knowledge and reasoning employed in the task.
- *Reflection* – the teacher provides opportunities for students to compare their own processes with those of the teacher, their peers and ultimately their internal model of expert performance.
- *Exploration* – techniques to make the student more autonomous, by forcing them into problem solving on their own. By the fading of support both for problem solving and for problem setting, the aim is to enable students to develop their skills of question setting and investigation.

The core elements of the approach are modelling, coaching, scaffolding and fading. This approach lends itself not only to teaching about the basic skills of using the computer as a tool, but just as well to the development of those skills to the level of use of the computer as a cognitive tool. As can be seen from the studies which Collins *et al.* considered from the domains of reading, writing and mathematical problem solving, the computer-as-cognitive tool approach can be used to model what it is to be a scientist or a writer or a mathematician. Much of the expertise inherent in these activities can be thought of as intellectual tools which the children can master using the apprenticeship model.

For example, the teacher can model a particular element of ICT at a technical level, such as how to carry out the 'cut and paste' procedure with a word processor. They would demonstrate where the commands were, in which menus, how to position the cursor, highlight the text and so on. This could be followed by a practice activity where the children attempted to cut and paste themselves, moving discrete words and phrases on the screen. This would be the scaffolding phase of the activity, with the teacher prompting them what to do, helping out as necessary, perhaps having supplied some crib sheets reminding them of the order in which to carry out the steps. Finally, there might be a sequencing activity where the children would use their new skills in context. The children could be presented with a familiar nursery rhyme but with the lines in the wrong order. They would then have to use the techniques of cut and paste to put the lines into the correct order. This would be the coaching phase, where the teacher observes the activity and prompts the children as necessary.

Now as well as learning the basic skill of cut and paste, at a later stage as part of learning to be writers, the teacher could model the editing process on the screen using that facility and again go through the scaffolding and coaching activities, but this time concentrating not on the technicalities of cut and paste but on its application as a technique for improving the writing process.

This model deals with that aspect of the learning environment to do with promoting higher order thinking, but there was also a hope of the transfer of learning to other contexts. Again ICT can offer opportunities for this. Salomon *et al.* (1991) draw an interesting distinction between effects with and effects of technology:

> We distinguish between two kinds of cognitive effects: Effects with technology obtained during intellectual partnership with it, and effects of it in terms of the transferable cognitive residue that this partnership leaves behind in the form of better mastery of skills and strategies.
>
> (Salomon *et al.* 1991 p. 2)

When considering the effects of technology, the idea of cognitive residue is interesting. A word processor has effects when using it in terms, for example, of the benefits for manipulating text, but the question is whether the use of the word processor leaves the child with any new knowledge or understanding of the writing process when away from the computer. This is what would be termed the cognitive residue of the activity.

The concept of cognitive residue relies on the assumption that higher order thinking skills that are developed during an activity can be abstracted and transferred to a similar situation. Perkins and Salomon (1989) suggest that general cognitive skills can be identified but that they always operate in highly contextualised ways using specific domain knowledge. They report that some studies show transfer of skills from using computer tools and others do not. It would appear that transferable effects can be achieved if that is part of the design of the teaching and learning process, but it is not an automatic consequence, it has to be cultivated. The activity, the goal, the teacher's role and the cultural setting must encourage what they term 'mindful abstraction' of the thinking skills and strategies used during the partnership with the computer. Making these principles explicit to the learner, decontextualising them and prompting for their use elsewhere can lead to their transfer to other activities. Perkins and Salomon (1988) offer some guidelines for classroom practices that can foster the transfer of knowledge and skills. Teaching for transfer can, in their phrase, 'get beyond educating memories to educating minds'.

This is the way that we mentioned in the section on LOGO, that generalised thinking skills might be developed as well as mathematical knowledge. De Corte (1990b) reports on just such a project using LOGO, aiming at the acquisition and transfer of general cognitive skills. Using the cognitive apprenticeship model they combined guided discovery learning with explicit teaching for transfer with some success.

The DfEE recently commissioned a review of research into approaches for developing pupils' thinking and one of the main conclusions is that what is needed is the development of what is termed the 'thinking classroom' where:

> high cognitive demand and challenge is embedded in a range of pedagogies which include – making thinking skills explicit within curricular content, focusing on talk and discussion about thinking, collaborative learning and maximising technological advances.
>
> (McGuinness 1999 p. 3)

These are exactly the ideas that we have been advocating in a range of ICT activities. Our thesis has been that what is needed is the creation of a culture in the classroom of learning about and talking about thinking skills no matter what the curriculum content, and that any number of ICT activities – the use of LOGO, working with information sources, engaging with simulations, developing semantic networks – can help in the creation of an environment for that culture to flourish (for further discussion of these ideas see Higgins 2001).

References

Abelson, H. and diSessa, A. (1981) *Turtle Geometry: The Computer as a Medium for Exploring Mathematics*, Cambridge, MA: MIT Press.

Bloom, B. (1956) *A Taxonomy of Educational Objectives: Cognitive Domain*. New York: Mackay.

Coates, D. *et al.* (2001) *Expert Teaching of Able Pupils.* Oxford: National Primary Trust.

Collins, A., Brown, J. S. and Newman, S. (1989) 'Cognitive apprenticeship: Teaching the craft of reading, writing and mathematics', in Resnick, L. B. (ed.)

Knowing, Learning and Instruction: Essays in Honor of Robert Glaser. Hillsdale, NJ: Lawrence Erlbaum Associates.

De Corte, E. (1990a) 'Learning with new information technologies in schools: perspectives from the psychology of learning and instruction', *Journal of Computer Assisted Learning* **6**, 69–87.

De Corte, E. (1990b) 'Towards powerful learning environments for the acquisition of problem solving skills', *European Journal of Psychology of Education* **5**(1), 5–19.

DfEE/QCA (Department for Education and Employment/Qualifications and Curriculum Authority) (1999) *The National Curriculum: Handbook for primary teachers in England Key Stages 1 and 2.* London: DfEE/QCA.

Eyre, D. (1997) *Able Children in Ordinary Schools.* London: David Fulton Publishers.

Freeman, J. (1997) 'Actualising talent: Implications for teachers and schools', *Support for Learning,* **12**(2), 54–9.

Gagné, R. M. (1982) 'Developments in learning psychology: Implications for instructional design; and effects of computer technology on instructional design and development', *Educational Technology,* June, 11–15.

Gardner, H. (1983) *Frames of Mind.* London: Fontana Press.

Ghaye, A. L. and Robinson, E. G. (1989) 'Concept maps and children's thinking: a constructivist approach', in Slater, F. (ed.) *Language and Learning in the Teaching of Geography.* London: Routledge.

Higgins, C. (2001 in press) *ICT in the Primary Classroom.* London: Falmer.

Jonassen, D. H. (2000) *Computers as Mindtools for Schools: Engaging Critical Thinking.* Upper Saddle River, NJ: Prentice-Hall.

Jonassen, D. H., Reeves, T., Hong, N., Harvey, D. and Peters, K. (1997) 'Concept mapping as cognitive learning and assessment tools', *Journal of Interactive Learning Research* **8**(3/4), 289–308.

Kemmis, S., Atkin, R. and Wright, E. (1977) How do Students Learn? Working Papers on Computer Assisted Learning. Occasional Paper No. 5. Norwich: Centre for Applied Research in Education, University of East Anglia.

Kozma, R. (1991) 'Learning with media', *Review of Educational Research* **61**(2), 179–211.

Laurillard, D. (1992) 'Learning through collaborative computer simulations', *British Journal of Educational Technology* **23**(3), 164–71.

McFarlane, A. (1997) 'The effectiveness of ILS', in Underwood, J. and Brown, J. (eds) *Integrated Learning Systems: Potential into Practice.* Oxford: NCET/Heinemann.

McGuinness, C. (1999) From Thinking Skills to Thinking Classrooms: A review and evaluation of approaches for developing pupils' thinking, Research Report No 115. London: DfEE.

Marcus, S. (1991) 'Technology, the gifted and the language arts' in Hoctor, M. (ed.) *Communicator: Teaching with Technology, The Journal of the California Association for the Gifted* **21**(1), 15–17.

Mercer, N. (1995) *The Guided Construction of Knowledge: Talk Amongst Teachers and Learners.* Clevedon: Multilingual Matters.

Mercer, N., Wegerif, R. and Dawes, L. (1999) 'Children's talk and the development of reasoning in the classroom', *British Educational Research Journal* **25**(1), 95–111.

Montgomery, D. (1996) 'Differentiation of the curriculum in primary education', *Flying High*, Spring, 14-27

Novak, J. D. and Gowin, D. B. (1984) *Learning How to Learn.* Cambridge: Cambridge University Press.

OTA (Office of Technology Assessment) (1988) *Power on! New Tools for Teaching and Learning.* Congress of the United States: OTA.

Papert, S. (1980) *Mindstorms: Children, Computers and Powerful Ideas.* Brighton: Harvester Press.

Pea, R. D. (1985) 'Beyond amplification: Using the computer to reorganize mental functioning', *Educational Psychologist* **20**(4), 167–82.

Pea, R. D. and Kurland, D. (1987) 'On the cognitive effects of learning computer programming', in Pea, R. D. and Sheingold, K. (eds) *Mirrors of Minds: Patterns of Experience in Educational Computing.* Norwood, NJ: Ablex.

Pea, R. D., Kurland, D. and Hawkins, J. (1987) 'Logo and the development of thinking skills', in Pea, R. D. and Sheingold, K. (eds) *Mirrors of Minds: Patterns of Experience in Educational Computing.* Norwood, NJ: Ablex.

Perkins, D. N. and Salomon, G. (1988) 'Teaching for transfer', *Educational Leadership* **46**(1), 22–32.

Perkins, D. N. and Salomon, G. (1989) 'Are cognitive skills context-bound?', *Educational Researcher* **18**, 16–25.

Polya, G. (1945) *How to Solve It.* Princeton, NJ: Princeton University Press.

Porter, L (1999) *Gifted Young Children: A Guide for Teachers and Parents.* Buckingham: Open University Press.

Rodrigues, S. (1997) 'Able students working in ILS environments', in Underwood, J. and Brown, J. (eds) *Integrated Learning Systems: Potential into Practice.* Oxford: NCET/Heinemann.

Salomon, G., Perkins, D. N. and Globerson, T. (1991) 'Partners in cognition: Extending human intelligence with intelligent technologies', *Educational Researcher* **20**, 2–9.

Schoenfeld, A. H. (1985) *Mathematical Problem Solving.* New York: Academic Press.

Skinner, B. F. (1976) *About Behaviourism.* New York: Random House.

Straker, A. (1989) *Children Using Computers.* Oxford: Blackwell.

Underwood, J. and Brown, J. (eds) (1997) *Integrated Learning Systems: Potential into Practice.* Oxford: NCET/Heinemann.

Wood, D., Bruner, J. and Ross G. (1976) 'The role of tutoring in problem solving', *Journal of Child Psychology and Child Psychiatry* **17**, 89–100.

CHAPTER 6
Conclusions

Throughout this book specific attention is given to the need to provide an enabling classroom climate to ensure that the needs of gifted pupils are met. The primary school experience should be about allowing children to discover their abilities and talents, as well as responding to those whose abilities and talents are already obvious. A curriculum focused approach to meeting the needs of the gifted enables schools to plan challenge for both those who they know will respond and also for those whose talents are as yet latent.

A differentiated approach to curriculum planning is the methodology stressed in this book. In each of the chapters the generic methods for increasing pace, complexity and abstractness are explored in relation to specific subject areas. In Chapter 2 differences are noted in the ways in which challenge might be presented in reading from the ways in which challenge might occur in writing. In both instances the same general themes are apparent, but their application varies according to the subject matter in question. Equally in Chapter 4, an enquiry based approach to science is stressed. In Chapters 2 and 3 enquiry is also a feature of extension planning but linked more closely to specific skill development.

In this book the need to take account of pupils' current level of attainment is regularly highlighted. As mentioned in Chapter 2, children coming into school can already exhibit significant skills or abilities. Formative assessment is therefore crucial to ensuring effective curriculum provision for gifted and talented children. Extension work is only challenging if it requires the child to operate in Vygotsky's zone of proximal development. Unless curriculum planning takes account of the child's level of understanding at the start of the module of a new area of work, the extension work can prove to be at an inappropriate level; either too easy or too hard. Formative assessment is therefore vital, but does not have to be arid. Chapters 2, 3 and 4 highlight ways in which the teacher can reach a judgement on a child's level of understanding through questions or games as well as by using more conventional methods.

A major challenge for the primary teacher in providing challenge for gifted and talented pupils is the range of subjects that need to be taught. Work with

Oxfordshire teachers (Eyre and Fuller 1993) highlighted subject expertise as a major concern for primary teachers. This book demonstrates for teachers practical ideas and strategies in individual subjects, both in those in which they may have significant expertise, but also and perhaps more significantly, in areas where they do not.

Research suggests that gifted pupils are at their most motivated when lessons provide a combination of new knowledge and an element of fun. Intellectual playfulness is at the heart of advanced cognitive thinking. The primary curriculum offers ample opportunity to combine these two elements. Children are being introduced to new knowledge, skills and concepts on a daily basis. In this book the need to make learning interesting is a recurrent theme. A wide range of examples are given of ways in which advanced work might be introduced in such a way as to make it challenging yet fun. ReCAP's research work has shown again and again that when primary teachers enjoy intellectual learning, and share that love with their pupils, then gifted and talented children thrive.

The main conclusion from this book is that by using a well-structured, curriculum focused approach to meeting the needs of the gifted, a school can make effective provision that can fit naturally with existing school provision and provide for precocious ability, as well as for latent ability. Much of what is recommended in this book could be used effectively with a wide range of pupils, including the gifted, rather than exclusively with a small sub-set of identified pupils. The ideas and strategies advocated stress the joy of learning and are designed to encourage children to strive in order to achieve highly. Finally, the approaches suggested do not intend to make the lot of the teacher more arduous and stressful, but rather to encourage schools to use good teaching skills to maximum effect.

Reference

Eyre D. and Fuller, M. (1993) *Year 6 Teachers and More Able Pupils.* Oxford: National Primary Centre.

Appendix One

BLOOM'S BUILDING BLOCKS

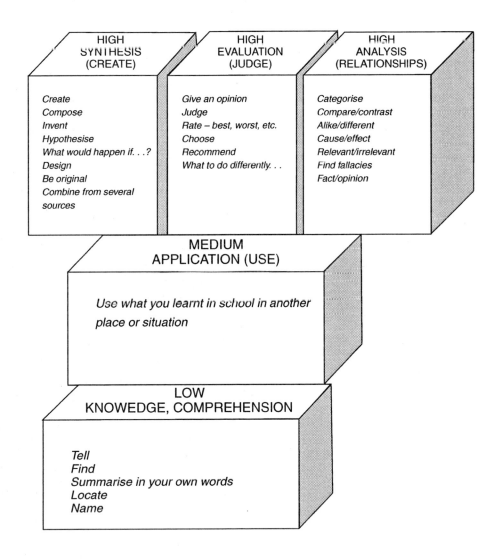

HIGH SYNTHESIS (CREATE)	HIGH EVALUATION (JUDGE)	HIGH ANALYSIS (RELATIONSHIPS)
Create *Compose* *Invent* *Hypothesise* *What would happen if. . .?* *Design* *Be original* *Combine from several sources*	*Give an opinion* *Judge* *Rate – best, worst, etc.* *Choose* *Recommend* *What to do differently. . .*	*Categorise* *Compare/contrast* *Alike/different* *Cause/effect* *Relevant/irrelevant* *Find fallacies* *Fact/opinion*

MEDIUM APPLICATION (USE)

Use what you learnt in school in another place or situation

LOW KNOWEDGE, COMPREHENSION

Tell
Find
Summarise in your own words
Locate
Name

(Adapted from Eyre, D. (1997))

Index

Printed in the United Kingdom
by Lightning Source UK Ltd.
109642UKS00001B/163-282